After Your Divorce

RebuildingBooks
Relationships – Divorce – and Beyond

After Your Divorce

Creating the Good Life
On Your Own

Cynthia MacGregor
Robert E. Alberti, Ph.D.

Impact Publishers®
ATASCADERO, CALIFORNIA

ATTENTION ORGANIZATIONS AND CORPORATIONS:
This book is available at quantity discounts on bulk purchases for educational,
business, or sales promotional use. For further information, please contact Impact
Publishers, P.O. Box 6016, Atascadero, California 93423-6016. Phone 805-466-5917,
e-mail: info@impactpublishers.com

Library of Congress Cataloging-in-Publication Data

MacGregor, Cynthia.
    After your divorce : creating the good life on your own / Cynthia
MacGregor and Robert E. Alberti.
      p. cm. -- (RebuildingBooks)
    Includes bibliographical references and index.
    ISBN 1-886230-77-3 (alk. paper)
      1. Divorce. 2. Divorced people--Psychology. I. Alberti, Robert E.
II. Title. III. Series.

HQ814.M237 2006
306.89'3--dc22   2005027719

Impact Publishers and colophon are registered trademarks of Impact Publishers, Inc.

Cover design by K.A. White Design, Templeton, California
Interior design by Sue Knopf/Graffolio, La Crosse, Wisconsin
Printed in the United States of America on acid-free, recycled paper.
Published by *Impact Publishers*, Inc.
POST OFFICE BOX 6016
ATASCADERO, CALIFORNIA 93423-6016
www.impactpublishers.com

Contents

Acknowledgments

With thanks to a marvelous co-author, easy and fun to work with, knowledgeable, and skilled at writing so as to blend his voice with mine — thank you, Bob Alberti.

— CM

It may not mean much to readers to know this, but Cynthia MacGregor and I have never met in person. We've worked together entirely at a distance by email, telephone, and mail (you remember the telephone and the mail, right?). It has been a unique pleasure to work with Cynthia. The idea for this book was hers, and I talked her into letting me share the fun. And it has been fun working with Cynthia.

We hope our readers find some fun here as well. Goodness knows, you need some fun in your lives after going through divorce.

I'd also like to acknowledge my late friend and senior co-author of *Rebuilding: When Your Relationship Ends,* Bruce Fisher, for expanding significantly my awareness and knowledge of the divorce process.

Finally, all those I've noted in the Dedication are due a major vote of thanks. Knowing we may have improved your lives a bit has been inspiration enough to keep at this work.

— REA

Foreword

YOU'RE ON YOUR OWN AGAIN with a chance to start over, to create your own good life.

Most folks view divorce as an ending — the ending of a relationship, of a marriage, of a recognized couple, of an intact family, of a two-parent household (if there are children), of life as you knew it.

But it's also a beginning — the beginning of a new life, a new direction, new opportunities to define yourself as an independent person. In short, the beginning of the rest of your life! And you can choose to *create the good life* for yourself — and your children, if you have them.

What *immediately* follows divorce is often tears, or a sense of relief, or maybe a mixture of both, along with a flood of other emotions. Depending on whether you sought the divorce or your husband did, and whether you were basically happy in the marriage or primarily dissatisfied (or flat-out miserable), the dissolution of your marriage may be a huge disappointment or a much-welcomed relief. You may be mostly happy or mostly sad.

Your feelings are very likely mixed. It's not easy to divorce someone you once loved — even if things went very badly toward the end. But now your marriage is gone, and it's time to get on with your life.

What's in Here for You?

We'll discuss your mixed emotions in some depth in the next chapter. But we're not going to stop there.

Books about divorce tend to fall into a few general categories. They may be about anger, ex-bashing and revenge, or about legal issues such as custody, or about forgetting the marriage ever happened, or about recovering emotionally. We're not going down any of those paths exclusively, although we'll have something to say about most of them. Instead, we hope you'll find this book a close friend and adviser on a wide variety of subjects as you create a new — and good — life for yourself on your own.

Just to be clear from the outset, this book is *not* about the actual divorce process. We're not going to help you wrestle with whether you should throw in the towel or keep trying, or any of the other myriad questions about the mechanics of getting a divorce or what leads up to it.

This book *is* about the practical aspects of getting on with your life, getting your life back on track, finding your way to new happiness — in short, creating the good life *after your divorce*.

We'll deal with both emotional matters and everyday matters — getting a handle on your roller coaster emotions, enlarging your field of interests, moving (or not), work, keeping or changing your job, helping your kids, making new friends, staying friends with people who are friendly with your ex, introducing your dates to your kids, money, and more.

Our Audience Is You

It's a ton of stuff to cover, so we've focused on a very special audience: women just like you. Rather than try to be "all things to all people"— divorced *and* widowed *and* separated women *and* men — we have deliberately aimed this book specifically at *divorced women*, not women who are thinking about divorce, or women who are widowed (though there is much in the book that widows may find useful).

No, we assume you've been there and done that. Your divorce is either history or well on its way, and this book is about what comes next. About getting your life back together. About finding happiness again. About dealing with all the questions and situations that come up along the way. And with just about everything else, up to the point you decide to get married again.

Of course, not everyone *does* get married again. And that's a valid choice too. You may prefer to stay happily single. "Happily" is the key word, of course. Or you may prefer to stay legally single, living with a special partner but not formalizing the relationship. And that, too, is a valid choice. We realize our readers will include both those whose beliefs — religious, ethical, or moral — preclude such a choice, and those who have no problem with a non-marital, living-together relationship. If something we say doesn't apply to you, just skip that part of the chapter. We're attempting to offer something to every divorced woman, and that includes a wide variety of people with a wide variety of values and attitudes and circumstances. If some of our ideas don't happen to agree with yours, we hope you'll stick with us anyway and draw on the material we've offered that you do find of help.

Problems with a Capital "P," and That Rhymes with "D," and That Stands for Divorce

Divorce brings its own set of problems and troubles — a truckload of them. Problems such as ex-husbands who want to reconcile; ex-husbands who object when you begin to date, or when they realize you are getting serious about some other man; ex-husbands who try to use the kids to spy on you; and more. Problems involving the logistics of shuttling kids between two homes. Problems of which parent pays for what. Problems of who takes care of the house now. Problems of buttinski friends and relatives who want to "help" by dissing your ex, fixing you up with a new guy every other week, advising you on everything from child care to auto mechanics to how to handle your ex.

Got children? We've addressed problems of single parenthood, including helpful material for readers who have children at home as well as for those women whose kids are now living with their father, or perhaps with Grandma or Aunt Kate. There are also segments of the book aimed specifically at divorced women with adult children.

No kids of your own? We recognize that many of our readers will be women who don't have kids at all, and we've included lots and lots of information that has nothing to do with being a parent

— single or otherwise. We each have grown children of our own, but we also know there is life beyond the rugrats.

We're going to make lots of suggestions, but we don't presume to know all the answers for *you*. Your life is your own, and if it sounds as if we're going too far at some points in the book, remind yourself, "These guys don't have to live my life. I'm going to do what's right for me!" (And that's a pretty good mantra for evaluating *anybody's* advice!)

We think you'll enjoy reading the stories of some women we know (or know of) who have been through what you're going through. Some of these are success stories. You may want to emulate what these women did. Some of these are failure stories. You can learn from those, too. But we do recognize — and celebrate — that not all women are alike, not all divorces are alike, not all ex-husbands are alike, and not all lives are alike. *You* have to weigh our advice and decide if it's right for you.

This book is not a pat, simple seven-step formula for the good life. There is no such thing (although Aristotle made a pretty good stab at it a couple of thousand years ago!). Divorce — and what comes after — is not a one-size-fits-all situation. In places throughout this book, we will raise questions to which only *you* can supply the answers. Sometimes knowing the right question to ask can be as valuable as knowing the answer.

We'll also offer, at the end of each chapter, suggestions for other resources, such as books and websites, from which you can get further help.

Who Are These Guys, Anyway?

You may be wondering just who "we" are, and what gives us the right to claim expertise about divorce. Let us give you a brief introduction to ourselves now:

Cynthia MacGregor, the author of over fifty books, is herself a "divorce survivor" and the mother of a grown daughter who also has "been there, done that, and brought home the T-shirt." Cynthia is the "go-to" person many friends call upon for advice. Many of her books have helped people — adults or kids — through difficult times. They include: *Divorce Helpbook for Kids, Divorce Helpbook for Teens, Jigsaw Puzzle Family* (all from Impact Publishers), *Why Do*

People Die, Why Do We Have to Move, Why Do We Need Another Baby, the *Abduction Prevention* series of six books, and many others.

Bob Alberti is a respected professional in the fields of personal development and divorce recovery — licensed psychologist and marriage and family therapist, consultant, author of a half-dozen books and editor of more than a hundred. He's been married — to his one wife — for more than forty-five years, but he's also a divorce survivor — his parents divorced when he was a youngster. He is semi-retired and works mainly as a book editor. Among his published works are *Your Perfect Right* (co-authored with Dr. Michael Emmons; 1.3 million in print), and *Rebuilding: When Your Relationship Ends* (co-authored with Dr. Bruce Fisher; over 900,000 in print).

One note of caution. The ideas we offer in this book assume you and your ex are pretty much mainstream, reasonable folks who just couldn't live together. We are *not* going to deal with the issues involved with a potentially violent, or actually violent, ex-husband. If you are dealing with such issues, although you surely need the information in this book, you just as certainly need far more help than we can offer you. And you need it *now*. Please contact — and stay in contact with — your lawyer, your local police department, and an agency in your area that specializes in offering practical aid to abused women. *Get local help*. Get it *now*. And keep it on your team.

And now, let's get down to it. Want to start creating your own good life? Read on!

After Your Divorce

PART ONE

Life on Your Own

1

●●●●●●●●●●

Getting Off
the Emotional Roller Coaster

OLD HANDS. FAST HEARTBEAT. Stomach upset. Headaches. Sound familiar? Like a roller coaster on steroids, perhaps?

No question. Divorce is a stressful time. Duh! In fact, it is second only to the death of a spouse in its stressful impact on our emotional and bodily systems, according to the most widely accepted measure of stressful life events.

Yet most folks try to go on as if it's "life as usual," taking no steps to deal with the inevitable emotional upset that a divorce — especially a messy, angry divorce — will produce. "Deal with it." "Suck it up." That's the popular wisdom — and it's dead wrong.

In this first chapter, we'll take a look at why, and what you can do for yourself about it — right away, during the first weeks after the breakup, and over the next couple of years, as you get on with your life after divorce.

Whose Idea Was This Anyway?

Whether the divorce was your idea or your ex-husband's, whether you chose to make the break or were the unwilling and unhappy recipient of papers he served on you, chances are that at first you'll find yourself experiencing a mixture of emotions, both positive and negative.

Even if you asked for the divorce, you may find yourself crying or feeling sad. Does this surprise you? It shouldn't. And it doesn't mean you're regretting your decision and wishing you were still married. You're going through a very natural grieving process. You're grieving for a dead dream. The wonderful marriage you wanted, and perhaps for some length of time actually had, or thought you had, doesn't exist. Gone is the dream, gone is the marriage, gone is any chance now that it might work.

You may have been the one who said, "I can't take another minute of this!" You may have complained to your friends that you had to get out of a bad (or simply unfulfilling) situation. But hope dies hard, and it's natural to hold on to a dream that things might still turn around, get better, and somehow work out. But once the marital ties are formally severed, and reality hits home that it really is over, even if part of you is rejoicing or feeling relieved, a part of you is likely sad as well.

You may blame yourself for the breakup — at least in part — even if in truth you were not to blame. (In most divorces, there is some blame on each side, though it may not be a case of fifty-fifty.)

Did he perhaps wander from the marital bed? Maybe he was abusive. Or perhaps he neglected or ignored you. Was he an addict, a gambler, a criminal? Do you find yourself wondering how you failed him, why he did what he did, what you could have done better or differently, so that he wouldn't have behaved as he did and things wouldn't end as they did?

Yes, usually there is some blame on both sides. Yet even when there isn't, a woman will still often blame herself. Even when the woman caters to the man, seeks help from a couples therapist to try to repair a failing marriage, does nothing to alienate him or cause marital discord, she may find herself asking: "How did I fail?" "What did I do wrong?" "What did I neglect to do that I should have?" Even when the man is abusive (and there is no justification for abuse, be it physical or emotional), she may wonder about her own "failures."

Though you may be glad and relieved that the marriage has ended, you might still regret the fact that it didn't work out as you'd hoped, and you may be blaming yourself for somehow failing to make it work.

But human emotions are funny things. Even if you're glad to be out from under, you may still find yourself crying a lot. And your friend Sally, who didn't want a divorce, may be experiencing unexpected happiness at times now that it's over. Despite the fact that she's sad, even crying over losing her husband to divorce, she may find herself feeling a surprising sensation of relief. Why?

You Didn't See It Coming — Or Did You?

Divorces seldom occur in a vacuum. Though it's not completely unheard of, it's relatively rare that a husband's or wife's request for a divorce comes totally out of the blue. Usually there's been some sort of marital difficulty, discord, or other unhappiness that led to the decision to divorce. Even if the couple didn't argue constantly, there were indications of discontent. When the divorce is final, the former couple has now become two single people again; the days of discord are finally behind them, and the woman may feel surprisingly relieved. She no longer needs to try to please the man she couldn't make happy. She no longer is struggling within herself to figure out what she's doing wrong. And of course, if there *was* fighting, it's over. Blessed peace and quiet has set in.

And even if she experiences loneliness, it's much less frustrating to be lonely when you're alone than to feel lonely within a marriage, as is often the case when a marriage is failing. When you're lonely and alone, it seems reasonable to feel that way. When you're lonely despite being in a marriage, it seems so wrong and unfair! And when you're lonely and alone, you feel you can take steps to remedy the situation; there's always hope for someone new and special in your future. But when you're lonely in a marriage, you feel very stuck in your situation, with little relief possible.

So it's no wonder that, even if the divorce wasn't your idea, and you weren't ready to give up on the marriage, you might find yourself experiencing feelings of relief and lightness of spirit now that it's over. Too, you've just been through a tense time. Perhaps your husband didn't move out immediately on announcing he wanted a divorce. Perhaps for logistical or financial reasons he remained under the same roof, whether he stayed in your bed or moved to the guest room. And then there was probably a certain amount of hassling and squabbling over the terms of the divorce: Who gets what, what the financial arrangements would be, and so on. So it's only natural that you would feel some relief or even happiness once it's over, things are settled, the divorce is final, and you can get on with your life.

Indeed, this is a time of tumultuous feelings. Please don't think yourself strange or unduly emotional or out of control if you cry one minute and grin the next, if you feel your world is falling to pieces even though you were the one who wanted the divorce, or if you feel a welter of emotions that run the gamut from down in the depths to up on the heights and back again. This is all very normal and usual...and this roller coaster ride *will* come to a stop.

On the other hand, you may find yourself feeling almost nothing at all. Some people's emotions go into a self-protective numbness. Not only don't you feel great emotion about the divorce, you don't feel much of anything about anything. Great good news barely touches you either. If you happened to hit the Lotto jackpot or learn that a professional association is about to honor you, you might barely shrug in response. Has your mind hit the "Off" switch on your emotions? This is just your mind's way of dealing with the hurt and confusion. And this, too, will pass.

Meanwhile, What to Do Now?

Until your life is more stabilized, there are things you can do for yourself that will help. And this is true whether you are feeling a riot of rampant emotions or a dull deadness of spirit.

❖ *Visit a friend you trust* and pour your heart out to her. Talk it out. You're not seeking advice now, merely a sounding board. (Of course if she gives you advice, and it feels like good advice, take it. But women, more so than men, understand that sometimes a woman just wants someone to listen, not necessarily to "fix it.")

❖ *Visit a "fun" friend*, someone with whom you can have a good time. Set aside your sorrows and your concerns in the company of someone who knows how to laugh (and how to make you laugh!), someone who's goofy or spontaneous or silly or otherwise fun to be with.

❖ *Go lose yourself in a movie, or read a good book.* (The early stages post-divorce might not be the best time to read a romance novel, though once you're past the initial hurt, a good romance, if that suits your taste in reading matter, might be just the ticket to remind you there are better things ahead for you.) As to movies, although anything you enjoy will likely be good for you, you have two best-case choices: a comedy or a three-hanky tear-jerker. Tears are cathartic, helping to wash away the hurt. A certain amount of crying is good for you. On the other hand, laughter soothes the soul. And, especially after you've cried and cried and cried some more, a diversion that takes your mind off how sad you feel and helps you laugh again is just what you need. Find ways to laugh and cry as you work through the loss of what has been.

❖ *Write* — a diary, or a journal, or some more literary form. Much poetry was born from pain, but even short stories, humorous essays, and other creative expressions can help get your feelings out on paper, help you work through what's eating at your heart, and aid the healing process. This is for you — don't even think about whether your opus might get published — if it helps you, it's accomplished a purpose. Indeed, if it's a diary entry, you don't *want* anyone else to read those very private outpourings from your soul.

❖ *Listen to — or make — music.* "Music hath charms to soothe...." Indeed it does. Music has charms, not just to soothe "the savage breast" but the wounded as well. Whether you're into country western (great sob music) or rock or classical or jazz or hip hop or reggae or some other type of music, and whether it helps you by bringing forth tears or by lifting your spirits, music is a wondrous healer. If you are talented enough to create your own music, so much the better!

❖ *Help someone else.* Helping others helps us in a multitude of ways. Most obviously, seeing others in need or in pain helps us realize that, however bad our situations are, others have it as bad or perhaps much worse. But on a less obvious level, helping others simply makes us feel good about ourselves. Your form of help could be volunteering at a soup kitchen or homeless shelter, working at a charity's thrift store, collecting for a fund-raising drive, doing the drudge work of mailing, filing, and such in a charitable concern's offices, working in your local literacy drive, helping through your church or synagogue, volunteering at your child's school, or helping at a local animal rescue project. The possibilities — and opportunities — are endless. On a more personal basis, you might choose to help one person or one family you know could use some help, be it respite care (short-term relief for a family caregiver), cleaning house for a harried and hassled mother of a large family, or cooking meals for an overworked and "culinarily challenged" neighbor. Whatever form of volunteer work you choose, you're not only doing good for the individual, or family, or community, you're doing good for yourself too.

❖ *Adopt an animal.* You have love to give. Especially if you have no kids, or they're grown and gone, a new pet to take care of (and to snuggle with) may be just the outlet you need for your love and your nurturing.

❖ *Return to your religious roots.* Some people feel marvelously grounded (and nurtured) by religion. Is that you? If you've drifted away from active membership in a spiritual community, consider a return. Was your break with the church or synagogue of your earlier years occasioned by some dissatisfaction with that particular congregation or its spiritual leader? Or was it the result of a disagreement with the tenets of that faith (or that denomination) itself? Try a different congregation, a different denomination, or even a different faith. Though you may have been a Baptist, you may find yourself more comfortable in a Presbyterian congregation, a Catholic church, or even a Jewish synagogue or a Unitarian meeting. Try getting re-involved in some community of faith. We're not suggesting a lifetime commitment here. Just go to services once. Try it on, see if it fits — and if it helps.

❖ *Get involved in something athletic.* Whether you join an amateur sports group — a locally organized softball league or regular volleyball game for adults, for example — or simply join a gym and work out, or sign up at your local Y or other recreational facility for swimming, physical exercise is good for more than cardio training and weight loss. It can actually help improve your state of mind!

❖ *Get involved in activities* to keep yourself busy and involved. We'll discuss some specific activities later in the book, as they serve more than one purpose. But for now, let's just say that instead of sitting home feeling sorry for yourself in your leisure hours, you can stop brooding about your situation by signing up for adult classes, joining a club, taking up a new hobby (or revisiting an old one), or doing volunteer work.

❖ *Redecorate your house,* or a part of it. You want to get past the initial upset (and shock, if the divorce was his idea). Nothing helps like a new beginning. Making a fresh start in some aspect of your life can help you feel that your whole life is getting another chance.

Sometimes a divorce results in the woman moving out of the marital home. Maybe she decides to move to another town in the wake of the divorce. Or maybe her husband got to keep the house as one of the terms of the settlement. Or perhaps it's financially unfeasible for her to keep up with the mortgage payments without a second income. Or there may be a hundred other reasons.

If you're staying put, some redecorating is in order. If you can't afford new furniture, how about new drapes or curtains? How about a fresh coat of paint for the living room, preferably in a new and different color? If you can't redo the whole house, how about a makeover for the room you spend the most time in, or the one that reminds you most of your ex? Did he spend most of his waking hours in the family room? It's time to give the family room an extreme makeover. Do you spend your evenings reading in an easy chair in the bedroom? Give that bedroom a new look that's all about you. Even a major rearrangement of the furniture can rejuvenate a room.

❖ *Seek professional counseling.* Some emotional upheaval, and some depression, is normal in the wake of such a life-altering event as a divorce. And most of us, in time, recover fine on our own… or, as the Beatles put it, "with a little help from my friends." But occasionally someone just can't shake the depression, or finds that the emotional roller coaster is non-stop, with no end in sight, or finds she is in such bad shape that she's unable to perform adequately at work or unable to do a good job of taking care of her family, or maybe even has suicidal thoughts. If any of these is true for you, it's time to look up a competent counselor. Seek out a psychotherapist, a crisis counselor, a clergyperson who's trained in handling emotional matters, or some other suitable professional. (If money is an issue, most communities have a free or low-fee community counseling center, or a university clinic, or an organization such as Catholic Charities or Jewish Family Services, which may be able to offer help on a sliding scale of fees. Start by calling the local crisis telephone service — often called "Hotline" — or your county social services agency and ask for referral to a low-cost counseling service.)

You Just Can't Trust Men, Right?

All right, we've talked about some of the emotions you're likely to experience in the immediate wake of the divorce, and some ways to cope with them. But those aren't the only emotional reactions you're likely to feel as a result of the divorce.

A mistrust of — or extreme anger at — men is a common reaction to the divorce process. Not every divorced woman experiences this, and those who do have these feelings don't all have them to the same degree. It's more common when the man was the one to ask for the divorce, but it also can happen when the woman was the "dumper," especially if she did it because of a trust issue (such as infidelity, dishonesty, or problems with gambling or other behavior that resulted in the husband misusing the family's money).

Janet, thirty-two, came from a stable family in which both her parents trusted each other and earned that trust. Janet met Dean while in college and married him shortly after graduation. Their nearly ten-year marriage had the usual bumps in the road any relationship is likely to experience, but overall it seemed solid. Janet and Dean had two children, to whom Dean was a good dad. There were no warning signals to alert Janet's "radar system." She thought everything in their marriage was fine.

Dean had a well-paying job with a fair amount of overtime, so his paychecks weren't consistent in amount. He handled their joint checking account, though the checkbook sat on the desk in the living room, so Janet was always able to see where the family finances stood. Janet deposited to the account her earnings from the part-time job she started after their younger child entered kindergarten. Though they certainly weren't rich, neither were they having to scrape to make ends meet.

The unraveling of Janet's marriage began when she and Dean decided to look for a larger house. Dean had always handled their tax preparation, so the actual amount of his income in any given year was not familiar to her. But now, discussing finances and mortgage payments with the mortgage broker, Janet began to hear some actual numbers, and something seemed amiss. When she did some calculations of her own, she realized Dean was earning considerably more money than he was depositing into the family's checking account.

The upshot of a long and, by turns, teary and accusatory conversation was that Janet learned — to her total amazement — that Dean was funneling off money from every paycheck to pay child support payments for a child he had fathered out of wedlock before ever meeting Janet.

Janet didn't know which upset her more: that Dean had been diverting money from the family regularly without ever telling her, or that he had another child but had never shared this information with her. "What *else* haven't you told me?" she demanded. And though Dean protested that he had no other secrets from her, her trust in him had been irrevocably shattered. The marriage faltered and fell apart as Janet found herself unable to trust Dean any longer. For his part, Dean was unwilling to admit that he'd done anything wrong. He assumed the stance that, since the family had enough money, and since the child was born of a relationship that was over before he met Janet, there was no need for her to know. In his view, Janet was the one making a big deal out of nothing.

Their decision to divorce was mutual, yet certainly not a happy one for either of the two.

Seven months post-divorce, Janet finally began dating again, but she found herself unable to trust any man. Even when her mother pointed out that Janet's dad was living proof that there are some trustworthy men in this world, Janet insisted ruefully, "They broke the mold after Dad."

In time, a woman in Janet's position might learn to trust again, especially if she meets someone open and trustworthy whom she really cares about. Till then, though, she's going to carry a heavy burden of skepticism and mistrust that will adversely affect any relationship she gets into. Or tries to get into, for how solid a relationship can you form when the underlying foundation of trust is missing? A woman who finds herself utterly unable to trust again would do well to seek counseling, although most such women do regain some ability to trust in time without professional help.

"I Can't Deal with This!"

Another common aspect of the post-divorce emotional roller coaster is a general inability to cope as well as before. With her nerves frayed and her emotions running high, a screaming child or a broken stove can be all it takes to set off a torrent of tears, or a wail of, "I can't handle it!" While there's no "insta-cure" for the problem, it should help you just to know that, first of all, what you're experiencing is pretty common and not a sign of weakness or failure, and second, this phase will pass.

Yes, you were used to having your husband help you, or at least provide a morale boost when things went awry, but your inability to cope now stems less from having to face things alone and more from just having so much heaped on your emotional plate. When your nerves are on edge and your whole world seems to have gone askew, one simple broken glass can be the proverbial final straw that triggers a torrent of tears and a feeling of utter inability to handle any sort of "situation."

But you will get through this phase, we promise you. Once you've accepted and become acclimated to the reality of your divorce, and you've begun rebuilding your life, you'll be handling small or medium-size day-to-day problems much more easily. And in the meanwhile, if you lose your temper more easily or feel defeated or scared more easily, don't be harsh on yourself for acting human. You're not the only woman who's having trouble coping with it all.

In fact, some people-watchers have figured out that a "female midlife crisis" is very common these days . . . other than simply those stresses brought on by menopause. We used to think of midlife crisis as a male phenomenon, usually involving young blondes and red convertibles. Now, it seems, a huge number of women admit to facing a "midlife crisis" quite apart from their menopause-induced issues. Sue Shellenbarger, in her recent book, *The Breaking Point,* reports that the number is around thirty-six percent of women in their late 40s and early 50s. That's more than the percentage of men who experience the phenomenon! You may not be that age, and your special stresses right now may have a lot more to do with your divorce than with the stage of life you're in, but if you're going through major emotional turmoil, you're dealing with the same sort of "turbulent psychological transition" Shellenbarger describes.

And if you *are* of a certain age, consider the double burden of your divorce together with the midlife issues. Perhaps you could forgive yourself for being a little edgy?

Divorced Again?

A song from several decades ago posited that, "love is lovelier the second time around." Many other things, too, improve as reruns, such as last night's leftover meatloaf, eaten cold on rye bread. But not everything is better the second time around...and divorce is one of these. The woman for whom the roller coaster is likely to be most difficult to endure is the twice-divorced woman. Already burned once in the divorce wars, she's going to be twice as crisped if she has the misfortune to get divorced again. And the effect on her still-at-home children is likely to be at least as devastating, if not more so.

The woman — and the children — enduring a second divorce are likely to feel more bitterness the second time around and to be less willing to trust. (And this applies not only to trusting a potential new love interest for the woman; it often carries over into a mistrust of people in general.) She may unconsciously withhold her emotions from someone wonderful in fear of getting hurt a third time. And her children may be just as unable — or even more so — to take a chance on loving yet another father figure.

Is there a magic "fix" to this problem? No. But recognizing what you are feeling (or what you are *not* feeling, but would like to be feeling) is a step toward correcting the situation. And time is still the great healer that often remedies the situation. There isn't always a perfect remedy. But sometimes, if you understand what you're going through, you can cope with it better. And sometimes, time alone will help.

What About the Other People in Your Life?

Children, parents, friends, neighbors, co-workers, bosses, group members, even casual acquaintances, can add stress to your post-divorce life. They ask well-meaning questions about "how you're doing" and expect you to give them all the juicy details. They offer to help, then don't show. They expect you to be your old self as if nothing had changed. They assume you'll fill in for your ex. And on it goes. We're not going to address those issues in this chapter, but have devoted several chapters in Parts Three and Four to the "People in Your Life."

Dealing with It in the Real World — Forget "Suck It Up"

There are constructive steps you need to take for yourself after your divorce, and we've outlined a few in this chapter. Look them over. All are proven valuable "stress fighters," but you probably won't find all of them appealing to you. We've also included some recommended resources where you can find out more about each one, should you wish to pursue it further. The rest of this chapter describes more tried and true activities that can help you to gain some ground on the emotional turmoil you've been experiencing, and to build a solid foundation for your good life.

More Help for Coping over the Long Haul

Earlier in the chapter, we offered a list of activities to get you started on your path to emotional recovery. Here are many more things you can undertake to stay on that path to the good life as time goes by.

❖ *Exercise* — You don't have to join a health club, or jog ten miles a day, but get off your duff and do something! Walk to work, or park your car at the far end of the lot and walk into the mall. Play tennis or golf, go bowling, ride a bike, swim, walk the dog, play physical games with your kids, do push-ups and crunches. Surf, ski, snowboard, take a hike in the mountains, chop wood, mow the lawn. Just as long as you keep moving and use your body. Somebody has recently suggested we need to take 10,000 steps a day, but who's counting? And make sure your kids are exercising regularly too! Get them involved in sports. Turn off the TV, the Nintendo and the GameBoy, and get them outdoors, doing the same activities we've suggested for you. Best idea: do it with them!

❖ *Watch your diet* — We're a fat nation. Obesity is epidemic and getting worse. If you're not part of the solution, you're part of the problem — for yourself and for your children. Pay attention to what you eat. Get off the fat track. Avoid fast foods, saturated fats, trans fats, fried foods, high-calorie foods, refined sugar, refined flour, high-fructose corn syrup — and too much of *anything*. Read nutrition labels. Eat lots of fresh vegetables and fruits, (and don't destroy the beneficial nutrients by overcooking the veggies). Eat whole grains, not white bread. Teach your kids good eating habits too. Avoid fad diets of all kinds: low carb, Atkins, Pritikin, South Beach, high protein, grapefruit....Stick with the tried-and-true "balanced diet." Watch your weight, but don't obsess over it. Watch your cholesterol, but remember that it's mostly hereditary. And re-read the section above on exercise!

❖ *Strengthen your support system* — Ultimately, we're all alone. At the same time, we all need the support and nurturance of others: family, friends, children, neighbors, co-workers, organization members, clergy, professionals. It's really important to have folks to turn to in a crisis, or even to share your joy. If you're in touch with family, stay in touch, and let them be an active part of your life. If you have good friends, nurture those relationships. It can be difficult to trust others with intimate details of your life, and we're not suggesting you wear your heart on your sleeve, but do allow others in where you can, and be grateful for their support and help.

❖ *Do lots of self-care* —Are you taking care of yourself, really? In addition to the ideas discussed above (exercise, diet, support), do you do things for yourself? We're not advocating selfishness, just nurturance. Keep in mind that if you don't take care of yourself, you won't have anything to give to others. You need to allow yourself time -- time for activities you love, time for quiet (meditation and reflection), time to be alone, time to be with those you love. And give yourself space as well -- space that nurtures you, space you can change to fit your mood, space that connects you with nature, private space that lets you do things you wouldn't do in front of others. "Hobbies" is a hackneyed concept, but get past the terminology and remember that what some call *hobbies* are simply activities that bring them pleasure. It needn't be stamp collecting, pottery, or restoring old cars. You can nurture your spirit by reading things you enjoy, hiking in the mountains, surfing, walking on the beach, doing needlepoint, playing an instrument, or romping with your dog. It's okay — even good — to pamper yourself a bit, also. Get your hair done. Buy a new outfit. (On a budget? You'd be surprised at what's available in the secondhand stores these days, often for a song!)

❖ *Learn to relax* — We don't mean vegging in front of the TV. We're talking genuine, deep, full-body relaxation here. This requires some practice, but you'll be amazed at how powerful a tool it can be when you're stressed. If you practice a regular relaxation routine for just a few weeks, you'll find you can apply it when you're in a custody hearing, or facing an aggressive landlord, or dealing with your ex or a difficult boss or co-worker. The process is simple: just learn what it feels like to completely relax the muscles throughout your body, and to breathe deeply. Then practice those deep relaxed feelings for twenty minutes a day, visualizing a relaxing scene at the same time. There are many relaxation/meditation tapes and CDs available, or you can simply sit or lie quietly and practice "letting go" of tension in each major muscle group (Start with your toes, and work your way up through your feet, ankles, calves, thighs, hips, lower back, upper back, shoulders, neck, chin, cheeks, and forehead, etc.) You'll need only a comfortable and quiet spot, and that hard-to-find twenty minutes.

❖ *Work on personal growth* — As you went through your divorce, you experienced lots of new emotions and circumstances for the first time in your life. You may have found yourself feeling powerless before the court system, unbelievably angry at your ex, frustrated with your attorney, frightened for your children… Those feelings are natural outcomes of a very stressful situation, and you don't want to ever experience them again. One way to minimize that possibility is to prepare yourself to handle anything life hands you with greater strength and self-confidence. There isn't room in this book to give you a full prescription for developing that strength and self-confidence, but let us suggest you look for opportunities to grow in several ways. Expand your education by taking night classes. Participate in personal growth workshops (try the local women's center, Y, adult education, or community college). Read a variety of self-help books. Learn to be more assertive and self-assured by taking an assertiveness or self-empowerment class. *Practice* what you learn — don't settle for making it an "academic exercise."

❖ *Take time to grieve the loss* — Famed divorce counselor and author Dr. Bruce Fisher said it takes a year or even two to fully recover from the loss of a love relationship. Have you given yourself time for that? Obviously it's different for each of us, but it takes *some* time for everyone. It is not helpful to "keep a stiff upper lip" and simply go on with your life. However resilient you may be (more on this in the following paragraph), you need to acknowledge the sense of loss and possibly failure and self-criticism that follow the breakup of an intimate relationship. Don't wallow in it, and don't treat yourself as if you're the only person who's ever gone through it. But do acknowledge the painful feelings and allow time for the action steps you need to heal your love-wound. And keep in mind that we're all unique, and some heal faster than others; the next section tells a bit about why.

❖ *Build resilience* — Recent studies suggest that some long-held ideas about recovery from traumatic life events may not be as universal as we had thought. It depends a lot on the individual, and it's very difficult to measure with any accuracy. For some, the trauma of divorce (or other wrenching life events) is devastating, leading to depression and great difficulty just getting through the day. It can take months or years for these folks to recover. For others, while the event is no less stressful, a level of personal "hardiness" or resilience comes into play, and they are able to cope, experiencing a much less destructive emotional response. Among the characteristics that seem to make the difference in bouncing back: successful experience with previous adversities, a solid support system, optimism, capacity for managing strong feelings (e.g., anxiety, anger), broad perspective (seeing "the big picture"), ability to plan and problem-solve. All of these are learned skills that you can develop.

❖ *Don't jump into a new relationship* — As you deal with the loneliness and emotional turmoil that you've likely experienced through your divorce process, it may be tempting to seek a new love relationship right away, to help you soothe the pain and get on with your life. Our advice, in a word: *don't.*

You really do need to take some time, even if you're one of the resilient folks who heal quickly, before you commit to a new love. Sure, there may be flirtations and brief romances along the way -- that's part of the healing process too -- but the best thing you can do for yourself at this stage is to get to know yourself as an independent person. Get your own life in order. Give lots of thought to your own goals (and those of your children, if you have them). In time, love may come again. If it does, you'll be ready. If it doesn't, you'll be ready.

❖ *Get help if you need it* — Don't be shy about seeking professional help if you're finding it hard to cope. Extended depression, feelings of hopelessness and helplessness, obsession with your former love, serious fears about the future...anything that gets in the way of your ability to get through the day is a possible suggestion to seek some form of counseling. In the Appendix, we've provided some helpful guidelines for knowing when you need special help, and how to find a professional who's qualified to provide it.

❖ *Take a parenting class* — If you're dealing with young kids as a single parent, you need all the help you can get. Parenting classes may sound a bit over the top if you've been at the business of parenting for a few years, but they can be a terrific source of information and support when you're juggling a job, a too-tight budget, too much month left at the end of the money, an ex, and a couple of youngsters.

There are lots of different approaches, but most classes will help sort out the issues of communication, effective discipline, sibling rivalry, misbehavior, quality time, special needs, and tips on giving your children the love and attention they need and deserve in the midst of your crisis. And the best part is that you'll discover you're not alone in wrestling with these problems -- all parents are facing them!

After Your Divorce — What's Next?

In this chapter we've begun to explore many of the steps you can take to get yourself together emotionally after your divorce. It isn't going to be easy, and it's going to take some time, but you will recover from the emotional disruption in your life.

Over time, you'll also gain the skills and independence you need to move ahead on your own successfully. In fact, you'll very likely surprise yourself with how well you'll handle the challenges of being on your own again. In the chapters that follow, we're going to present many more ideas that we think you'll find helpful in that process. Stay tuned!

AfterWords — Chapter One

Key Points in the Chapter

- Regardless of which of you initiated the divorce, you're most likely experiencing a mix of positive and negative emotions. That's normal!

- There are many things you can do to help yourself get through this emotional time. Among them are talking with a trusted friend, writing in a journal, listening to or making music, helping someone else, playing sports, talking to a counselor.

- You can learn to trust men again, though it may take some time.

- It may seem you just can't cope right now. Be assured: This phase will pass.

- Among the steps you can take to help yourself cope: Exercise, watch your diet, build your support system, learn to relax, work on personal growth, take time to grieve, don't jump into a new relationship, get help if you need it.

Activity of the Week

- Check your local library or favorite bookstore for an audiotape, CD, or book with detailed instructions for deep relaxation or meditation. Spend at least twenty minutes a day in a quiet place, practicing a relaxation exercise. (Yes, you can. You'll gain back more than the time spent!)

_____   _____

Suggested Readings and Resources

Ahrons, C. (1994). *The Good Divorce.* New York: HarperCollins.

American Psychological Association (2004). *The Road to Resilience.* Washington, DC: APA. (Free brochure. Order at www. apahelpcenter.org)

Berry, D. (1998). *The Divorce Recovery Sourcebook.* Los Angeles: Lowell House.

Bloomfield, H., Colgrove, M. & McWilliams, P. (1976, 1991). *How to Survive the Loss of a Love.* Los Angeles, CA: Prelude Press.

Everett, C. and Everett, S. (1994). *Healthy Divorce.* San Francisco: Jossey-Bass Publishers.

Holmes, T.H. and Rahe, R.H. (1967). The Social Readjustment Rating Scale. *Journal of Psychosomatic Research,* (2) 213-228.

Shellenbarger, S. (2005). *The Breaking Point: How Female Midlife Crisis is Transforming Today's Women.* New York: Henry Holt & Co.

Walton, B. (2000). *101 Little Instructions for Surviving Your Divorce: A No-Nonsense Guide to the Challenges at Hand.* Atascadero, CA: Impact Publishers.

Webb, D.W. (1999). *50 Ways to Love Your Leaver: Getting On With Your Life After the Breakup.* Atascadero, CA: Impact Publishers.

2

•••••••••

Climbing the Mountain of Divorce Recovery

F AMED DIVORCE THERAPIST Dr. Bruce Fisher of Boulder, Colorado, spent more than twenty years working with people going through the divorce process, and he developed and refined a step-by-step process for emotional recovery. Bruce died in 1999, but his nineteen-step "rebuilding blocks" model — which he compared to climbing a mountain — has become the most widely recognized standard for the recovery process and has benefited more than a million recently divorced folks around the world. The most common reaction when divorced people read or hear Bruce's insights? "How does he know exactly how I'm feeling?"

We encourage you to read Bruce's landmark book, *Rebuilding: When Your Relationship Ends* to get a complete view of each of these vital steps in the pain and recovery process. (Full disclosure: Dr. Bob co-authored *Rebuilding*, so the process described in that book helped to shape this one, but it was Bruce Fisher's creative energy and research that developed the rebuilding concept.)

Here's a very brief summary of the process, describing the emotional downward slide and upward climb that almost always happens over the year or two following a painful divorce. You will probably be able to locate yourself along the "trail," and that should be some help in recognizing the emotional recovery work ahead for you.

Denial — "I Can't Believe This Is Happening to Me." At first, you just can't believe it's happening. Your marriage had a few problems, but certainly not enough to cause a break-up. Now he's gone, but it must be temporary, right? Surely you'll work it out and get back together.

Fear — "I Have Lots of It." But what if you don't "work it out"? What if you really are alone and getting a divorce? Can you live with it? What a scary thought...not having him to talk with, to turn to in time of trouble, even to argue and fight with. How will you ever get along by yourself? What will you do?

Adaptation — "But It Worked When I Was a Kid!" In the early years of your marriage, you figured out how to get along with him. It was much as it had been at home, with your parents and siblings. You had to deny your own feelings at times, but you adjusted, you *adapted*. But it turned out that adapting was not enough. In fact, it didn't work. You changed yourself so much that you forgot who *you* were, what *you* wanted.

Loneliness — "I've Never Felt So Alone." If you're like most young marrieds, you probably never had much time alone, never found out how to get along in the world by yourself. Did you go from home to school to college to marriage seamlessly, without time to find yourself as a separate and unique individual? Now you must face the world alone. Maybe you come home to an empty apartment. Maybe your family is hundreds of miles away. Not so much as a dog or cat for company. Whom can you talk with? Whose shoulder can you cry on?

Friendship — "Where Has Everybody Gone?" Friends? What friends? Suddenly all the people who were your "friends" have disappeared. They're couples, remember? It's uncomfortable having you around as a single. Maybe they'll try to pair you up for parties, but they sure don't seem very supportive or available these days. But friends are important, and a key goal at this stage is to develop new relationships and build a support system.

Guilt/Rejection — "Dumpers 1, Dumpees 0." When he left, you were devastated. Or maybe you left and he's the one crying a river. Either way, it's pretty common for the "dumper" to feel guilty, the "dumpee" rejected. This stage of the process can last a while, because the dumper often wants to deal with his guilt by "helping" the dumpee feel better. That usually makes things worse.

Grief — *"There's This Terrible Feeling of Loss."* You've lost so much. The closeness, the love, the dream, the partnership, the home, the image...There's a ton of grieving to do, and it doesn't happen fast. "Helpful" friends and family will tell you to "get over it," but it doesn't work that way. Facing it, accepting it, and working through it take some time.

Anger — *"Damn the S.O.B."* Divorce anger is like none you've ever known. Bruce liked to call it "angerism," to point out how unusually powerful this feeling is, particularly for the dumpee. Divorce attorneys love to harness this feeling, because it can really boost their fees! "We'll fix him for what he did to you!" And all the while the meter is running.

Letting Go — *"Disentangling is Hard to Do."* Now you're starting to turn the corner. You've allowed yourself to acknowledge that it's over. You're starting to think about yourself, and where you go from here. You're giving up the false hope of reconciliation. You're getting realistic about the future.

Self-Worth — *"Maybe I'm Not So Bad After All!"* While you're in the divorce pits, it's pretty hard to see yourself as a person of value, of worth. You may have blamed yourself for the end of your relationship, or at least wondered what you might have done differently to save your marriage. Now you're beginning to realize that the breakup was not all your fault, and that you're every bit as good a person as anyone else. And you can accomplish something with your life, even without him.

Transition — *"I'm Putting Away the Leftovers."* As you start to believe in yourself again, you realize you have to give up the emotional baggage of the past. Lots of who you are has been based on who you were as part of a couple. Now that's behind you, and you're beginning to let go of the "leftovers" that tie you to the past.

Openness — *"I've Been Hiding Behind a Mask."* Gradually, you're admitting that you've probably not been very honest with the world. Like most folks, your "public face" is quite different from who you are inside. Could it be time to let that mask slip and risk really being yourself as you begin to create new relationships?

Love — "Could Somebody Really Care for Me?" Ooooh…this is a scary one. Even the thought of loving again, taking the risk of making yourself vulnerable, is enough to send you back to the safety of your private space. Yet if you're risking the "real you" with others, you're very likely finding that others like what they see, and some are even attracted romantically. It's exciting, scary…Time to go slowly.

Trust — "My Love-Wound Is Beginning to Heal." As good things begin to happen to you, as you reach out to others and they respond favorably, you're finding that the scar from your breakup is less tender. You're not quite as afraid to trust someone with your feelings. You may even begin to find yourself attracted to those who trust you in return. Could there be room in your life for romance again?

Relatedness — "Growing Relationships Help Me Rebuild." "Dating? Me? I don't think so! But maybe coffee…or a group activity…well, there's no harm in going out to dinner, I suppose…." Casual relationships can begin to seem okay, and there may even be a "lasting" romance on the horizon. Indeed, you do need to risk connecting again, but it's not quite time for lasting love. Romance at this stage is best seen as a "transitional" relationship, for learning and growing in your ability to love again.

Sexuality — "I'm Interested, but I'm Scared." This is a tough one. You have needs. Everybody does. Yet you don't want to jump into bed too casually. You're probably not ready to commit to an intense long-term partnership, but you do need physical closeness. This area has strong moral overtones for many folks, and premature sexual involvement can sometimes signal a commitment that neither partner is ready for. Lots of open communication needed here.

Singleness — "You Mean It's Okay?" Millions of people do get along alone. You don't have to be half of a couple. Family, friendships, career, community activities, sports, politics, hobbies…there are tons of ways to find fulfillment in life apart from romantic partnerships. Being single can be a rewarding and meaningful life, and many find it freeing, allowing them to pursue career and personal interests that would be extremely stressful for married folk.

Purpose — *"I Have Goals for the Future Now."* If you've come this far on your path of recovery from the breakup of your love relationship, you very likely have thought a lot about where you go from here with your life. You've probably developed a strong sense of what you want in a future love partnership, or in your career, or in the larger society. Or you may intend to devote yourself entirely to your children.

Freedom — *From Chrysalis to Butterfly.* This is the end of the recovery road, and the beginning of "the rest of your life." You're free of the bounds of past relationship, you've become an independent and self-assured woman who knows what her goals are. No, you're not perfect, but you're ready to move on and perfect yourself!

After Your Divorce — What's Next?

In this short chapter, we've just begun to explore many of the steps you can take to get yourself together emotionally after your divorce. It isn't going to be easy, and it's going to take some time, but you will recover from the emotional disruption in your life.

Over time, you'll also gain the skills and independence you need to move ahead on your own successfully. In fact, you'll very likely surprise yourself with how well you'll handle the challenges of being on your own again. In the following pages, we're going to present many more ideas that we think you'll find helpful in that process.

P.S. If you think Bruce Fisher's "rebuilding" model sounds like something you might like to experience for yourself, check out www.rebuilding.org for a seminar location near you.

AfterWords — Chapter Two

Key Points in the Chapter

- There are many steps to full recovery from the end of a love relationship. Drs. Bruce Fisher and Bob Alberti have described nineteen such steps in their book, *Rebuilding: When Your Relationship Ends* (third edition).

- It can take a year or two to work through your divorce process.

- Steps in the "rebuilding" process include: Denial, Fear, Adaptation, Loneliness, Friendship, Guilt/Rejection, Grief, Anger, Letting Go, Self-Worth, Transition, Openness, Love, Trust, Relatedness, Sexuality, Singleness, Purpose, Freedom.

Activity of the Week

- Re-read this chapter and consider each of the nineteen "rebuilding blocks" identified in the Fisher-Alberti model.

- Think about your own process of divorce recovery. Where would you place yourself on the climb up the "mountain" of rebuilding blocks?

- Find a small notebook or journal and sketch out a plan for taking the remaining steps in your divorce recovery process.

Suggested Readings and Resources

Fisher, B. & Alberti, R.E. (2000). *Rebuilding: When Your Relationship Ends* (third edition). Atascadero, CA: Impact Publishers.

Fisher, B. & Bierhaus, J. (2004). *Rebuilding Workbook*. Atascadero, CA: Impact Publishers.

www.rebuilding.org

3

• • • • • • • • •

Big Changes in Your Life

L
OTS OF FOLKS FIND CHANGE UNCOMFORTABLE. But change often can be a distinctly good thing. Divorce is certainly a major life change, and it can be good for you!

Women have long been the subject of jokes (mostly by men) about their propensity for rearranging the living room furniture. Though sometimes such a change is called for by practical necessity (is the sun fading a fabric?), often it is the result of a woman's frustration with her life. If certain aspects of her life are unsatisfactory, and she can't do anything about them, she can always rearrange the living room furniture and feel she has control over *some* aspect of her life. She's able to make *something* in her life better.

But for every woman who gains the illusion that moving the sofa is making a change for the better in her life, there is another woman who is loath to move it, even if the move will hide an ugly red wine spill. Change is very upsetting for many people — even a relatively minor change like repositioning a piece of furniture. There is something very comforting about the status quo. What's familiar is reassuring. And what's new and different can be unsettling at best, scary at worst.

Which accounts for a portion of the discomfort that comes with divorce. In virtually every case, there are many more changes involved in divorce than just the absence of your ex-husband. And, for those of us who don't take changes easily, the onslaught of so many of them is an occasion for great stress.

What can you do about it? Well, you can't easily make yourself over into a person who embraces change. And you can't alter the fact that there are many changes in your life in the wake of the divorce. But you *can* recognize the changes in your life and admit that, for you, changes are stressors. It also helps to realize that this reaction to change is common and widespread and does not signify a weakness on your part. Many, many people don't handle change well. But sometimes just identifying a problem is half the battle of resolving it. If you recognize and accept that this is part of why you feel uncomfortable, you can begin to feel less so.

There are *some* things you can do to help yourself. Let's start by taking a look at some of the changes that go along with divorce.

New Schedules

One change you've noticed immediately is that your daily schedule is different. Maybe you planned your dinnertime around the time your husband got home from work. Did you usually have dinner on the table when he came home? Or maybe a half-hour later, so he could change clothes or take a shower or have a drink? Now you don't need to have dinner at 5:30 or 7:00 every night. You can eat when *you* want to, or whenever you find it convenient.

Of course, if you have kids at home, you need to take their schedules into account. You don't want to serve dinner after your five-year-old's bedtime and thus keep him up late. You don't want to put your eight-year-old to bed ten minutes after he gets up from the table. If your fifteen-year-old has evening band practice, you'll need to allow enough time for her to get to practice without having to gulp her dinner to keep from being late. And if your life revolves around two or more children, you're probably a pro at juggling the dinner hour.

But, within certain boundaries, you can eat at your own convenience now. And that should feel liberating. For some people, though, this kind of freedom is far from being liberating — it's downright scary. If it's scary for you, and you can admit that, you're on your way to doing something about it. As a next step, think about the benefits of this new flexibility. Keeping your own schedule is a *good* thing. You could work out after work, go for a drink with "the girls" from the office, stay late to finish a project so you don't have to go in early tomorrow, or take in the "early bird" special at your favorite diner.

Speaking of food, if there were foods your husband wouldn't or couldn't eat — foods he disliked or was allergic to or otherwise was restricted from eating — you're free to cook and eat them now!

Other aspects of your routine may be different as well. If the times you'd been getting up in the morning and going to bed at night were for the convenience of his schedule more so than yours or your kids', you may find yourself getting up earlier or later, going to bed earlier or later, or doing other things on a different schedule. Did you both shower in the morning? Now you no longer have to be out of the shower by 6:15 so he can take his shower on time. You may be able to sleep fifteen minutes longer!

You may find yourself going to bed later just to avoid the empty bed. Or, if the two of you squabbled a lot, and you tried to avoid being in the same room with him as much as possible, you may find yourself going to bed earlier, now that the bed is no longer a battleground to be avoided. Such changes, while welcome, may still be unsettling. Take a deep breath....

Your Ex Has Exited

Maybe your husband was in the habit of doing a lot of the family cooking. Now you don't have that help; you have to do it all yourself. You're too tired after a day at work, your kids need your help with their homework, the phone keeps ringing and demanding your attention, the dog has knocked over the flowerpot and created a terrible mess (there's no husband to help you with that, either), and you don't know which direction to run first. This is definitely a change, and it may be hard to find the bright side. The absence of a partner for help in dealing with everyday occurrences is a change that's tough to adapt to, for more reasons than just because it's difficult to cope with change. There are real, practical reasons why this change is rough on you.

Time for an Extreme Makeover?

Did your husband take some of the furniture with him when he left? Is his absence all the more pointed because his recliner is so obviously missing from the living room? Does the empty space in the den where his pool table used to sit give you a pang? In fact, you may be relieved that he's gone...but, once again, these differences in the look of your home point up the fact that there's been a major change.

Emily and Rob had been bickering and squabbling for over a year. Though there had been no major blow-ups, life was a constant battle. He was the one who finally said, "We'd be better off apart," but Emily didn't disagree. In fact, she was relieved when he moved out. There were times when she missed him, and there were times when she missed some aspects of married life (which is not the same thing as missing the man himself). But overall she felt it was for the best that they had agreed to get divorced.

She had mixed emotions, which is very normal. "You're starting over!" her best friend, Cara, told her. "Why don't you redecorate the house? Make a *real* new beginning!"

Emily thought that was an excellent idea. She would do the house over as much as was practical. It would signify a fresh start. "Out with the old. In with the new!" she declared.

Reasonably handy with a paintbrush and not afraid to climb a ladder, Emily repainted the living room herself…not just a fresh coat of paint but a whole new color scheme. Now instead of four beige walls she had three off-white and one robin's-egg blue.

Emily had the living room sofa and chairs reupholstered, bought new drapes, and replaced the carpet with ceramic tile. She kept the knickknacks that had special meaning for her but got rid of the others and bought some new decorative accents. Since she had no luck with plants, yet liked having greenery around the house, she bought five artificial plants. (Rob had always derided imitation greenery, but he wasn't around anymore!)

In the bedroom, she painted the walls a deep rose and bought a new bedspread and curtains to match. Though she didn't replace any of the furniture, she did move all the pieces around. She also bought all new sheets and towels.

She expected to feel wonderful as the result of making such a clean sweep and fresh start. Instead, she reported to Cara, "I feel lost. It doesn't feel like my house anymore."

For some people, making changes in the house, whether it's new paint, new drapes, new furniture, or just a rearrangement of what you've already got, can be a great signal that "things are going to be different now," and can provide a much-needed boost. Others can't handle too much change at once; they prefer to keep their surroundings as the one stable thing in their chaotic lives.

Changing Your Address?

When Lizbeth got divorced, she found it necessary to move from her spacious, expensive apartment to a more modest place. Her mother offered to help furnish the new apartment with new things "so you'll feel like you're getting a real new start," but Lizbeth wisely asked her mom not to do it.

"Can I take a rain check?" she asked. "Maybe in a year or so I'll be ready for new furniture and stuff, but right now, I think my old things will be a comfort to me."

Lizbeth was wise. She recognized that she was a person who found changes a bit rough to take, and she knew that the divorce and the move were two major changes already. She realized that having her old furniture and other familiar objects around would make her new place feel like home. And even when her mother insisted, Lizbeth prevailed. Her state of mind was much the better for having her old comfortable things in her new apartment and new circumstances.

Moving is certainly a major change. And there are many reasons that you might have to move — or simply choose to move — after your divorce:

❖ You may need to move to a less expensive home or apartment if you don't feel financially able to maintain your present home. The housing market in many parts of the country today has made it very difficult for many families to find decent affordable housing.

❖ You may choose to move from a house to an apartment so a superintendent can handle the needed repairs and maintenance of the building, heating and air conditioning, landscape, pool, and fences.

❖ Your husband may, in the divorce settlement, get the house you had lived in together (especially if the court determines that he's going to have residential custody of the kids).

❖ You may wish to move out of a house that holds bad memories for you.

❖ You may elect to move out and get away from "wagging tongues." Maybe there was a lot of gossip in the neighborhood centering around your divorce, or the circumstances that led to the divorce. Or maybe the divorce was the result of your husband's affair with a neighbor, who still lives down the block or in your apartment building. It's certainly understandable that you might wish to move to get away from her.

❖ You might have lived in your home out of your husband's choice, not yours. Now that his choice is no longer relevant, you'll want to move. Perhaps he wanted or needed to live close to his work, or near his sick mother. Or perhaps you were a one-car family, and so you located yourselves within walking distance of the train station. Now that his wishes or needs are not important, you may want to move to a neighborhood nearer to your work, your family, or your friends.

❖ Maybe you'd like to have the kids in a better school district, or just one that you like better.

❖ You may be starting a new job as the result of the divorce and want to live nearer to that job. You may move out of town altogether. Perhaps there's a job offer in another city that you now feel free to take.

❖ You might want to move nearer to your mom or sister or cousin, so that they can be on call for family emergencies, or for after-school babysitting, or just close by to offer moral support.

❖ You may even elect to move in with someone else — your parents, another relative, a friend, another single mom, another divorcee with no kids — for a variety of reasons: economic necessity, having a housemate who can help with the kids, companionship, or other considerations.

❖ If your husband has moved nearby, you may want to move to distance yourself from him, particularly if he's in any way abusive — physically, verbally, or emotionally. This may mean moving across the country or simply across town. You may not wish to leave the area — and in fact your divorce decree, if there are children involved, may specify that you have to stay within a certain area — but even if you can't leave town, you can still move to another neighborhood, so that you're not shopping at the same stores, patronizing the same bank, or otherwise likely to run into each other.

❖ You may wish to move just for that feeling of a fresh start. If you are not one of those people who get thrown off-kilter by changes (or maybe even if you are, as long as you are cognizant of what the move may do to you), starting over in a new house or apartment, a new neighborhood, or even a new city with a new climate and new surroundings may be just the right thing for you. Did you always want to live in the warmth of Southern California or South Florida, in the mountains, or at the seashore? Maybe now's your chance!

But beware of moving away from your support network. Even a move to another neighborhood in the same town can be problematic if your mom, your sister, or your best friend has been your neighbor up till now, and you're used to being able to run next door when you need two eggs or a shoulder to cry on. If your kids are at an age where they can stay home alone as long as they know that Grandma or Aunt Louise or best-friend Debra is right next door, that will be hard to give up.

A move to another town takes you even farther away from your support network. Long distance calls might be free on your cell phone, and e-mail is a wonderful thing, but there are times when you can't replace physical proximity — such as when you urgently need a hug and some basic comforting. There are times when you need more tangible help, whether it's a free babysitter or at least one you feel comfortable with, or someone who can help you with your clogged rain gutters. You'll have to start over to develop those resources in a new place.

Remember too, you're still you, and you're not likely to change who you are and how you relate to others *just* because you relocate. You'll take your *self* with you wherever you go, and you'll very likely deal with folks *there* just as you have dealt with folks where you are *now*. Think about how tough it is to change habits. Think about how tough it is for someone who goes off to a retreat to stop smoking or drinking or whatever, then comes back to the same neighborhood and house and friends and family. Bingo! Right back into the old habit again.

A move to a new home is probably the biggest change outside of the split-up itself that a divorce can bring, but it is certainly not the only change. What are some of the others, and how will they impact on you?

Money Changing

Take money. Now, there's a subject that seems to command everyone's attention.

If you have minor children and they are living with you, you almost certainly were awarded some amount of child support in your divorce decree. Additionally, you may have been awarded some amount of spousal support as well. Yet it is highly unlikely that the amount of money you now have coming in will allow you to live on the same budget level as when you were married.

This will bring about a variety of changes, from changes in your employment situation to changes in your lifestyle. Were you accustomed to eating out often? You may be cooking at home most nights now. Were you accustomed to fine foods and wines? You may now find yourself searching the Internet for creative new recipes for ground hamburger or pasta, and sipping bargain-store soda instead of special wines with your dinners.

In cases like this, it is not simply the fact that things have changed that is tough to deal with. The actual changes themselves are what upsets you. Similarly your next vacation may involve taking a train trip to visit your cousin in Boise instead of jetting to Cancun to stay in a luxury hotel. A night out may mean pizza and bowling instead of going to an expensive night spot. And trips to the mall may feature only window shopping, rather than spending your now-meager cash reserves.

Changes with the Children

If you have young kids, you will have to say "No" to them more frequently, too, which may be even more difficult than denying yourself the luxuries you now miss. And it may be harder for them to understand. Typically, they'll want to blame someone, either Daddy for leaving or you for asking him to. No matter how angry you might be with your ex (for leaving or for his behavior that led up to the divorce), it accomplishes nothing positive to encourage the kids in this type of thinking. Don't egg them on to blame Daddy because they can't have a new video game or motorized scooter or pair of trendy sneakers. Not even if you yourself feel the blame should fall fairly on him.

This doesn't mean *you* should be the scapegoat. In deflecting blame from your ex, don't encourage the kids to blame you. Rather, try to help them to see that not everything in life has to be someone's fault. (This is a good lesson for them to learn anyhow.) Often in life, circumstances are not what we want them to be, through nobody's negligence or misbehavior. That's just the way things are. And we have to deal with it. If you set a good example by dealing with the changes in your circumstances as a result of the divorce, you're in a better position to help the kids understand that this isn't "Daddy's fault" or "Mommy's fault" or *anyone's* fault. In other words, "stuff happens."

Other changes may impact on the kids too. They may, for example, have to undertake more chores around the house and yard, especially if they're older. Their allowances may be cut back by your budget cuts. Allow the kids a reasonable amount of griping; it's natural for them to express themselves. (Be honest: Haven't you complained to your friends that you hate not being able to afford that new outfit or having to give up your housecleaner or having so little money for food anymore?) Allow them to get it off their chests, and sympathize. But help them to learn not to go on and on and on with their complaints. You can tell them, "Okay. I hear what you're saying, and I understand, but that's the way it is now. We have to live with it, and get on with our lives" — or words to that effect.

This is a good time for them to learn that *doing something* about a situation is better than just complaining about it. It's also a good time for them to learn to distinguish between situations they can help or change and ones they can't. Short of money? Wanting something they can't afford on their reduced allowance or something you can't buy them on your reduced budget? Maybe they can earn money from a sidewalk sale of old comic books, books they've outgrown, or unwanted toys or games. Perhaps you could hook them up with eBay, help them build an old-fashioned lemonade-type stand, or introduce them to a local consignment shop.

Or they might be able to earn money by doing chores for neighbors. Are your kids old enough to rake leaves, weed gardens, mow lawns, shovel snow, babysit, or do other odd jobs for people in your block or building or cul de sac? (Caution here: check out potential "employers" before sending your kids out to strangers' homes!) Inspire the kids with a good capitalist work ethic: Work and you'll earn. You *do* have some control over your own fortunes.

Their reduced financial situation can lead to a great lesson in economics and the value of work. It's up to *you* to help them get the lesson and turn this change in the family's fortunes into a learning and growth experience for them.

More about dealing with your kids' needs in chapters 7, 8, 9, and 10.

Who Are Your Friends?

We're not yet finished with the changes in your life that may come about as the result of a divorce. What about your friends? Further along we'll discuss finding and making new friends. For now, suffice it to say that you may want to meet some people who are:

❖ Not friends of your ex

❖ Not half of a couple

❖ Single-again (as opposed to never-married)

❖ In similar financial circumstances to yours

❖ Interested in some of the same things you are.

And you may want to have less to do with some of your old friends, especially if they still see your ex-husband socially. (Not that that's a reason to drop a friendship, but you may be less comfortable seeing them socially and talking frankly with them now.)

Now that you're no longer half of a couple, you may have more in common with people from your office or from your field of work. Seeking out people with whom you share a work connection is especially likely if you're returning to work after quitting to raise your kids. This is true whether you've returned to your pre-marriage career or have changed careers.

Another change in your "friendships," although surely a smaller one, is that you may adopt a pet for the first time. Perhaps, now that you live alone, you want a dog for security, or a dog or cat for companionship. (If you haven't thought about it before, consider it now.) Or maybe your husband was allergic to pets or simply didn't like them. Now that this roadblock no longer exists, why not consider adopting a Rover or a Fluffy from a local humane society or animal shelter? (Hopefully you'll find a more creative name than those old chestnuts!)

Now, That's Entertainment!

Your preferred form of entertainment may change too. We've already discussed finances as a reason why your nights on the town may morph into pizza and bowling. Your being solo, not half a couple, can change other things as well. Were you used to playing bridge as a couple and now you're without a partner? Till you find another bridge partner you're happy with, bridge may be out of the picture. Were you used to sailing on weekends, only now your ex has custody of the boat? You might go sailing with friends or, if your weekends on the water were more a matter of habit than a great love of sailing, you might skip it altogether. Were you accustomed to going camping because that's what *he* liked? If it's not your "thing," you need never crawl inside a sleeping bag or tent again!

Your new interests may lead you in new directions. Have you reverted to an old hobby? Maybe you'd abandoned writing poetry for years. Why not see if there's a "poetry slam," poetry open mike night, or poets' discussion group at a local coffee shop, library, or bookstore? Have you recently taken up painting? See if there's an artists' support group nearby, or a group that gets together to paint companionably and offer each other help.

And There's Always the Small Stuff

You may find other changes in your life too. You may trade in your old vehicle for a more reliable one or a less expensive one with lower payments or better gas mileage. Or, if you're not a mom (or your kids are grown and gone), you may want to drive something sporty and flashy, a convertible perhaps, symbolic of your new independence and freedom.

Similarly, you may find yourself changing your style of dress, your hairstyle, even the way you apply your makeup. Sometimes a makeover is just the thing if the divorce has left you feeling "dumped" and unappreciated. (Even if you were the "dumper" and not the "dumpee," divorce can do a number on your ego and leave your self-esteem on shaky ground.) But a makeover, altering your appearance, can do wonders for your psyche as well. You can affect a different look or become a different person.

Have You Changed, Too?

Remember that down deep underneath you're still you, no matter what external changes you accomplish. This is said as a comfort, not as a caution. Too much change can be frightening. Yet we understand that you may not *want* to be *exactly* the same person you always were. You may wish to become a more educated person, a more interesting person. You *can* undertake these changes, or others. Just keep in mind that you're not really a different person entirely; you're just *a different version of you.* Your core values, your core good qualities, your essential beliefs all remain. You're still the person you were; you're just a *new and improved* version.

You can peel off the veneer of the married woman, the veneer of the woman who goes to boat shows to be a good wife, the veneer of the woman who entertains her husband's business contacts out of necessity but really is uncomfortable doing so. You can add a layer of new independence, perhaps sophistication, new interests, perhaps a new career (and the new self-confidence that sometimes brings). But you're still you underneath.

Don't try to change yourself *too* much. Now is a time for good changes *if* you handle changes well. Take your changes in small increments. Don't overdose on them. You're more likely to be successful in your efforts to change if you go about it in small steps. This is not the time for an "extreme makeover."

Remember, changes are stressors. Whether or not you stress out from a small change, almost everyone will get stressed from too many changes at once. So be careful about adding additional stress to your life at this already-stressful time by trying to become "someone new," or making a major career change, or relocating to "get away from it all," before you've worked through the divorce recovery process.

Changing yourself takes a lot of work. This book gives you lots of tips for that work, and lots of resources to guide you on your journey to becoming the person you want to be on your own.

Take it slowly...take it easy. And take it on your own terms.

Work?

Maybe you've noticed that we've come to the end of this chapter about changes and haven't discussed work or career. Because of their importance, we've devoted a whole chapter to those topics. It comes up next.

AfterWords — Chapter Three

Key Points in the Chapter

• The major life changes that come with divorce can be as stressful as the divorce itself, or more so.

• Common areas of change include schedules, losing your ex's help with everyday activities, home furnishings, moving to a different location, finances, parenting, friends, entertainment... even yourself.

• Many changes will happen whether you want them or not, so you may wish to keep some things the same... daily routines, or activities, or your living environment. It's important to maintain some stability and familiarity in your life at this stressful time. Take it slowly.

Activity of the Week

• In your journal (notebook), jot down a list of things that have changed, and things that have stayed the same, since your divorce. Examples:

Where you live	Transportation	Your appearance
Home furnishings	arrangements	Who lives with you
Children's school	Discipline	_____
Neighbors	Your health	_____
Household budget	Your attitude	_____
Friends	Work	_____

• Highlight or check those items that are particularly stressful for you now.

• Think about and write down ways you can ease the stress. (E.g., get help with a problem item, learn to relax, make adjustments to minimize the problem, talk to a therapist....)

• Create a step-by-step action plan to deal more effectively with the changes in your life.

Suggested Readings and Resources

Berry, D. (1998). *The Divorce Recovery Sourcebook.* Los Angeles: Lowell House.

Parents Without Partners:
   www.parentswithoutpartners.org/about.htm

www.Divorcecentral.com

4

• • • • • • • • • •

Your Working Life

"**W**ORKING MOMS" IS A POPULAR TERM for women who have both children at home and paid employment somewhere else. But did you ever know a mom who *didn't* work? Sure, plenty of women are stay-at-home wives and mothers (though because of the cost of supporting a family these days, that number has decreased dramatically). They're still "working women"; they just don't get *paid* for their labors.

Divorce multiplies the financial stresses on families, of course, and it often puts stay-at-home wives back into the workforce. Your employment situation may be due for a change, too.

We've emphasized the fact that too much change all at once is difficult for some people to cope with, and the wake of a divorce may not be the best time to make other sweeping changes in your life. And yet, that said, sometimes it's a good thing indeed to make some changes, then step back and see what other aspects of your life could use improving.

You know yourself better than anyone else does. Can you handle change well? Or is change a tough thing for you to cope with? If you haven't made many other changes (such as moving to a new home), it may be a good idea to let your fresh start include more than just the divorce, such as finding a new job.

If you are already employed, you may need to switch from part-time work to full-time, or from one job to two. It may not be necessary, though, to work extra hours in order for you to earn that additional money you now need. Changing from one job to another might do it. Could you be earning a substantially larger salary at a different firm in your field? You may like the company you work for, and you may have been there for many years, but maybe it's time to make a change.

If the cost of childcare practically wipes out any salary you could realistically expect to earn at your level of skills and education, how about work you can do at home? (For example: taking care of other people's children in your home; buying and selling on eBay; starting a small business you can run from home; creating and selling your art or craft handiwork; sewing or crocheting or knitting new clothes and selling them through local shops; making alterations to garments for customers; telephone sales; keyboarding or other services for small businesses.)

Beware of leaving secure employment in a solid company for either self-employment or employment in a firm with a shaky future, where you might be downsized (or the company could go out of business altogether). If your divorce has left you in a strained financial position — as is often the case — this is not the time to take a huge risk. Consider carefully the possibility of a negative outcome from a job change before you take that step. (And watch out for scams like "Make money stuffing envelopes at home!" The only folks who make money on those "jobs" are the ones who sell the scam to you.)

If you need more flexible hours so you're available for your children, you may have more options than you think. Have you asked your boss about the possibilities? Can you afford to cut back to three-quarter time (for example, six hours a day)? Can you do a split shift, so you're home more when the kids are? Can you work two part-time jobs, such as prep cook and waitress? Is a career change possible — one that would allow more flexibility?

Rethinking Your Career

Perhaps you'd do better not just in another company but a whole new field where your same skills are also needed. Maybe it's not your hours or your company but your job or your field that needs to change. How about a completely different job for which you have the requisite knowledge and/or skills? When was the last time you checked the job market? Don't get stuck in a rut and think that just because you've always been a medical transcriber or an interior designer, that's what you are and that's that. Divorce is about changes. Maybe it's time for a career change.

And increasing your income is not the only reason for changing careers.

Paula, married, thirty-two, and childless by choice, was dissatisfied with her life. Her biggest area of dissatisfaction centered around her marriage. It wasn't an intolerable situation (her husband wasn't abusive, nor did they argue constantly), so she'd been telling herself maybe she was expecting too much out of marriage. She tried to make do with the life she had.

Finally, she came to a point at which she realized she really did need to put an end to her marriage. It might not be intolerable, but it wasn't making her happy. She felt she deserved better.

Once she realized she wasn't chasing a Cinderella dream, but was entitled to some real happiness, she divorced her husband. She found that living alone, while it had its lonely moments, really was better than living in an unsatisfying marriage. And now there was a realistic hope that things would improve, that she would meet someone better somewhere down the road.

And yet, Paula realized her life still wasn't as good as she'd like it to be. At first she chastised herself for chasing rainbows. She had a nice apartment, good friends, a secure job that paid a reasonable salary...what more did she want? Did she really have the right to expect more?

And yet, the lesson she had learned by getting out of her marriage stayed with her. She *could* make her life better. What was it that still seemed to need improvement?

Paula decided it was her job. She was going through the motions, but she gained neither satisfaction from the work itself nor appreciation from her boss. There had to be something better out there! She wanted a job that allowed her to be more creative and to have more contact with people.

She learned that a local non-profit agency was looking for someone with a skill set that Paula felt she had: preparing publicity materials and supervising volunteers.

Although the job was totally different from anything Paula had ever done, and she did not have any background working for a nonprofit, she felt confident she could handle it. She faxed her resume to the number in the ad, followed up with a phone call, landed an interview...and got the job!

And she really loved it. In the space of just a few months, with the divorce and the job change behind her, she felt she had turned her life completely around. "I've reinvented myself," she told her sister.

Of course Paula hadn't really reinvented herself at all, but she *had* reinvented her life, and definitely for the better.

Paula was really fortunate, of course. Faxing a resume rarely even gets you in the door. Landing a new job takes lots of work. You'll have to identify prospective employers, locate openings, find out what kind of application is required, arrange for an interview, show your stuff, and follow up persistently. In short, finding work can be a full-time job. But you can do it!

What's Out There for You?

"Think outside the box" has become popular advice.

What would you *like* to do if you could have your choice? What interests you? What do you think you would be good at? Browse through the Sunday paper's "Help Wanted" to get ideas. Bookstores and libraries have long shelves of resources about career growth and change (we've listed a few in the Resources section at the end of this chapter). You might want to visit with a career counselor at the local community college.

If you don't have the necessary skills to significantly improve your income through a job change, maybe it's time to go back to school. Again, "Think outside the box." Get beyond such negative ideas such as, "That's a ridiculous dream," or "I could never get that job," or "I can't go back to school now."

"Education" doesn't necessarily mean four years of college. There are technical and vocational schools and community college programs that can train you for a new career. There are two-year associate degrees. There are colleges that will give you credit for life experience and skills. And there are colleges that give partial or full scholarships to "non-traditional" students. Think you're too old because you're not eighteen and just coming out of high school? Did you know that the average community college student today is nearly *thirty years old*? (More about education in the next chapter.)

Your life experiences can serve you well in the workplace, too. If you've got a background in volunteer work at a charity, homeowners or neighborhood association, or the PTA, the skills you learned —

from directing a staff of volunteers to writing press releases — may be just what you need to snag a job. Even your experiences running a household have probably taught you to supervise, multi-task, organize, delegate…skills that come in handy around an office. You may be great material to become an administrative assistant, a supervisor, or a customer relations specialist.

Co-Workers in the Real World

What about the people you encounter at work? Chances are you have a pretty good handle on the various personalities at your current job. But what if you change jobs? You don't know what the people at your new job will be like. This is not to say you shouldn't change jobs. Nor is it to say that you won't or don't have any negative encounters with your current co-workers. But the folks where you work now know you and are less likely to give you the sorts of problems that can beset divorced women in the workplace.

What sorts of problems might you encounter?

Certainly the "office wolf" is an annoyance. Yes, you can complain about sexual harassment, but who wants to go through all that? Then there are the women who see you as a threat because you're single. If they're single too, they may think of you as competition for whatever eligible men they may have their sights set on, whether it be co-workers, customers or suppliers. Then there's the office gossip mill — although, realistically, the staff of your current workplace is probably more likely to wag their tongues over your divorce than is the staff of someplace new, where your fellow workers never knew you as anything but divorced.

None of this is a reason *not* to change jobs, but it *is* a heads-up that the odds of encountering bozos, and behavior you won't like, are at least as great if you change jobs as if you stay put.

And here's another thought: If you previously worked from home (and childcare is not a concern), you may now want to seek out a job that requires you to work on-site. You trade the comfort of a "commute" from one room to another, and the conveniences of your home at hand, for the liveliness, stimulation, and companionship of being out in the world working with others. In fact, you may want to "trade up" to a job among more people even if you weren't previously working at home. Is your current job in a small office or shop with little traffic? If so, think about whether you'd like to work in a larger office with more people around you. Or maybe you'd prefer a sales or customer relations job, or some other type of job where you meet members of the public.

A friend of Cynthia's took a weekend receptionist job, in addition to her good Monday-to-Friday job, despite having the skills to command a single, better-paying job. She was divorced and wanted to get out and meet people, and a front-desk position afforded her that opportunity.

Rona, another woman we know about, works in a small office Monday through Friday with mostly older women. She doesn't get much companionship or outside exposure from that job, but she loves her work, makes good money, and wouldn't consider quitting. Since her ex-husband has their children all day on Sundays, Rona took a Sunday job as a "greeter" at a car dealership. It's not a sales job — it's actually more like being a receptionist — and the pay isn't great, but it provides her with more "people time" and gives her the opportunity to meet new folks.

Getting Ahead in Your Career

Now that you're supporting yourself — and perhaps your children — it's more important than ever to advance your career whenever and however you can. When you are employed, don't overlook on-the-job training opportunities offered by your employer. Take advantage of evening courses, weekend workshops, and other educational programs that will advance your career and earning potential. You could move up, and perhaps work fewer hours for more money.

How you work is likely to make a difference also. If you're an employee, work as if you owned the business. If you own your own business, treat yourself as well as you would an employee.

Unless there are union or company or government rules about "who does what" on the job, pitch in to do what needs to be done. Don't wait for a custodian to empty the trash. Don't ask someone else to make your calls. Don't call maintenance to turn off a faucet (unless it's leaking!). Do ask what you can do to help. Pitch in and do the obvious without being asked, especially if you work in a small firm. Your initiative will be noticed, and an enlightened employer will reward it.

Can You Do It All?

If you're worn out from juggling the demands of career and family, be assured you have plenty of company. In her recent book, *How She Really Does It*, TV producer Wendy Sachs notes that even "successful" working moms — many of them famous, with lots of cash to throw around — frequently wrestle with guilt and have trouble finding time to do it all and still sleep a few hours. She suggests that moms seek flexible work hours, or consider working at home, to help balance the conflicting demands.

Not everyone can do that, of course. Try waitressing from home, driving a school bus, working on a highway crew, or teaching third graders.

Be careful about overdoing it. The "great American malaise" of overwork is real. Maintain a good balance between your work and your personal and family life.

Keep in mind that a job or career change by itself is not likely to be your golden key to the good life. Check it out carefully before you jump!

AfterWords — Chapter Four

Key Points in the Chapter

- Divorce is likely to change your working life in important ways. You may take a new job, seek advancement, change jobs, work outside the home for the first time, start your own business, move to flextime, or even change fields.

- Advanced education or specialized job training may open opportunities you didn't even know existed before.

- Co-workers may or may not be supportive as you go through your divorce recovery process. Potential problems: ostracism, gossip, sexual harassment.

- You may find it helps to take a job where you'll meet lots of new people.

- Consider flexible hours, or part-time work, working at home, or other ways to balance work time with family time and personal needs.

Activity of the Week

- Spend time this week reading the classified "Help Wanted" ads in your local newspaper. Note the number of jobs and local companies you hadn't heard of before.

- Make a list of jobs that sound interesting to you.

- Go online, at home or at the public library, and do a "Google" search on at least three different jobs you identified in the steps above. Write down in your journal the qualifications required, the career opportunities in the field, and what appeals to you about it.

Suggested Readings and Resources

Bolles, R.N. (2005). *What Color Is Your Parachute? A Manual for Job Seekers and Career Changers.* Berkeley, CA: Ten Speed Press.

Krumboltz, J.K. and Levin, A.S. (2004). *Luck Is No Accident: Making the Most of Happenstance in Your Life and Career.* Atascadero, CA: Impact Publishers.

Phelps, S. & Austin, N. (2002). *The Assertive Woman* (fourth edition). Atascadero, CA: Impact Publishers.

Sachs, W. (2005). *How She Really Does It: Secrets of Successful Stay-at-Work Moms.* Cambridge, MA: Da Capo Lifelong Books.

5

• • • • • • • • • •

Broadening Your Horizons

W E'VE MADE THE POINT that change can be hard to handle. Divorce is nothing if not about change. But divorce can also afford you the opportunity for some good changes. Sudden change, or unexpected, unwelcome, unwanted, or multiple changes simultaneously, can be very rough on you indeed. But not all change is like that. Changes that take place gradually and voluntarily — from within — don't result in the same shock to the nervous system.

In fact, this *may* be a wonderful time for you to make certain changes in your life. Handled carefully, any time is a good time to evolve and grow. We all need to keep growing and improving as we go through life. Being in a new situation — divorced and on your own again — you may be in a particularly good position to benefit from cautious changes in your life.

Changing does not have to mean reinventing yourself. If you're thinking that it may be time for a major "personality overhaul," or that your values or beliefs are overdue for a shake-up, we'd advise caution. This may not be the time for such significant disruptions. You have some exploring to do before you're ready for that. (Take another look at chapters 1 and 2.)

But if you're happy with who you are — your values, your beliefs, your inner self — then consider how you might improve on that foundation. Have you thought about changes in your career, your appearance, your finances, where you live, your interests...maybe your education?

Back to School?

In the previous chapter, we briefly touched on education as it relates to getting a different or better job. But not all education is for the sake of improved employment. Education has many purposes and values. For example, knowledge for its own sake, learning new practical skills, keeping your mind active and involved, knowing more about other cultures, understanding political and economic factors that affect us as citizens, looking at the world through different lenses, and sheer enjoyment are important and valid reasons for continuing your education.

Seeking more education can also be a great excuse for simply getting you out of the house. Not a very elegant or intellectual reason for taking classes, perhaps, but a very human one. Are you restless but don't quite know what to do with yourself in the evenings? Or, to the contrary, do you realize you're housebound, yet too comfortable to break out of your lethargy and do something? You know you'd be better off getting out there, being among people, doing something more than reading or watching TV or doing the crossword every night. How about signing up for a course somewhere?

Don't be put off by the prospect of formally enrolling in college. Not all education is found within ivy-covered walls. Consider these possibilities:

❖ non-credit courses at your local college.

❖ instructional television programs in your area (often under the auspices of the local school board, sometimes broadcast on public television stations or on dedicated instructional channels).

❖ online courses sponsored by for-profit or not-for-profit schools, professional societies, corporations and others, usually completed at your own pace, and available on virtually any topic you can think of. You can even get a formal university degree online, from some of the nation's most respected institutions!

❖ "community education" or "adult education" courses, usually offered in the evening, at your local public schools.

❖ YMCA, Jewish Community Center, or similar groups, or through the leisure activities department or recreation department of your town.

❖ local coordinating group (sometimes called an "open university," or "learning center") that publishes lists of classes, signs up interested individuals, charges a fee for each class, and retains a percentage of the tuition to cover costs.

Another advantage of continuing education is that classes (except TV and online) are a great way to meet people. Often single-again women ask, "Where do I go to meet men? I'm not into the bar scene." One of the answers is *classes*. In most classes, you'll meet both men and women. Of course not all the men will be single, or the right age, or of interest to you. But that's true no matter where you go. Even singles clubs and singles dances attract their share of married cheaters posing as singles. And just because a man is single and the right age, that doesn't mean he's going to be "your type." But if you're both taking the same pottery class, photography class, conversational Italian class, or defensive driving class, you at least have a common interest…and isn't that a good start?!

Expanding Your Social Circle

"Meeting people," of course, doesn't only mean meeting men. As a divorced woman, you're probably interested in connecting with other women who are also divorced, widowed or unmarried. Even if you're still comfortable talking to your married friends and socializing with them, they don't share your circumstances, and you'll likely be happier having at least a few friends who are also divorced as you are and can relate to the situations in which you now find yourself. Married friends are not likely to appreciate the pitfalls and joys of being single again, the hassles of getting your ex to pay the child support on time, the heartbreak of trying to comfort a child who's crying for her daddy, the logistics of cooking for one when all your recipes serve four, or the anxiety of being only one parent when it's time for both Sean's soccer game and Chelsea's 4-H meeting.

You may already have single or single-again women friends from work or from the neighborhood, but there's hardly such a thing as having too many friends. Friendship is a great source of support, comfort, advice and information, and it doesn't hurt that your single friends may also be a good source of introductions to single men!

Where else can you meet new friends and/or new men? One popular answer is at the gym. Another is at a club that focuses on specific hobbies and special interests. Akin to classes, but not so structured and formal, there are countless clubs or groups that meet to engage in a shared interest, be it bird-watching or body-building, photography or pottery, quilting or scrapbooking, model boats or flying kites. Many such groups are sponsored by an organization such as the local YMCA or Jewish Community Center, or perhaps a church, synagogue, or mosque. Others operate independently, and you may have to ask around a bit to find them. (Check your local newspaper or rec department.) All offer opportunities to engage in a hobby or pursuit that interests you, or one you'd like to learn more about, while meeting new people.

Many religious congregations have women's clubs, men's clubs, and singles clubs. Some even sponsor groups specifically for divorcées or for over-thirty-five singles. (The Rebuilding seminars mentioned in chapter 2 are often sponsored by churches.) Joining a church or synagogue can also help you meet new people, even if you don't join the women's club or singles group.

The congregation can be an extended "family" for your kids, too. Right now they probably feel their family has shrunk a little. Even if they see Dad three days a week, he isn't there full-time. A religious congregation can help toward making them feel something's been added back into their lives.

Whether or not you have kids, religious organizations offer many opportunities beyond worship services that will get you out among people. You might choose to volunteer for a community service project, sing in the choir, teach religious education classes, work on a committee, or help out in the youth department.

Volunteering

While we're on the subject of volunteering, don't overlook charitable organizations as a means of broadening your horizons, meeting new people, and even acquiring new skills. Whether it's a local charity or the local branch of a national cause, and whether you're wearing fifteen different hats while helping run a three-person office, or tightly focused on one task as a small cog in a huge agency full of many people, your talents will be welcome.

It's an opportunity to learn new skills, too. Never planned anything larger than a child's birthday party before? You may help in planning the foundation's annual gala... and you may be able to turn that newly acquired skill of party-planning into a marketable asset later on when you're job-hunting or starting a new business of your own. Never supervised a staff of people before? If you find yourself rising in the ranks of the charity, with fifteen people reporting to you, you may be able to list that on a resumé at a later date.

Want something more strenuous? Check out the volunteer opportunities at your local chapter of Habitat for Humanity, the international organization that builds affordable housing for needy families — primarily with volunteer labor. No experience necessary!

Or maybe you'd just like to find out what you can do.

Elena, a talented writer who had never pursued writing as a career, was also handy at crafting decorative works. When she was married, she created and sold decorative wall hangings. Since her husband's substantial income was more than adequate to support the family, she chose to stay home and work on her projects rather than join the outside workforce. Her only child was already in college.

Elena volunteered for the local Neighborhood Betterment Association, where she was put to work at a variety of tasks. One of these was editing and designing the association's newsletter. With her flair for writing and her eye for design, she seemed a natural. Just one problem: She wasn't familiar with the computerized graphics program in which the newsletter was created. Fortunately, one of the other members gladly taught Elena how to use the program, and in a short while she became proficient at it.

Then came the divorce. Her husband's midlife crisis had brought an unexpected end to their marriage. Elena realized she would need to go to work, but she didn't think she had any marketable skills. She had never sold her writing, and she didn't have a college degree. Now in her late forties, she realized the odds were stacked against her if she competed for jobs with journalism school grads in their twenties. What to do?

The answer came when a friend mentioned that a real estate management office was looking for someone to produce newsletters for the many apartment buildings the company managed. With her skill at writing, Elena had that part of the job aced, but the friend pointed out that she would need to be able to design a newsletter using a computerized graphics program, too.

"I can do that!" Elena exclaimed. "I learned how at the Neighborhood Betterment Association!"

As it worked out, that wasn't the only skill Elena had developed in her volunteer work that helped her get the job, but it was the clincher. Volunteering not only had broadened her horizons but also led to a job that paid a decent dollar.

That's a classic example of "doing well by doing good." While Elena was bettering her neighborhood, she was also bettering herself. And while her volunteer work started before her divorce, yours can well begin afterward.

In the meantime, you're out of the house, doing interesting things that keep your mind sharp, meeting new people and having new experiences, and not sitting home feeling lonely or sorry for yourself. And, since you're working for a charitable organization, you can pat yourself on the back for the good you're doing the world, or a corner of it. Won't *that* make you feel great?

Where to start locating a volunteer group that could use your help? Try the local newspaper's "volunteer opportunities" section, check out the bulletin board at your library, or listen to the "community calendar" listings on local radio or TV. Maybe your town has a volunteer fair. Many non-profits have tables at local farmer's markets or other community-wide events. Ask around at your kids' school, or at church, or the city recreation department. There may be hundreds of volunteer opportunities in your town or nearby.

What about community social and service organizations? There are literally dozens of service clubs and other groups, many with both women and men members, some with affiliations to men's organizations, some related to career fields, some related to religious faiths, others with a service motive, and most are wide open to new members. Check out local chapters of major political parties, or environmental action groups. Each plays a unique role in the community, each has a diverse membership, most have both men and women members, and all offer many opportunities to expand your horizons.

You'll probably find many of these are contributing in a community near you:

Library volunteers or "friends"

Service clubs (Lions Club, Rotary, Soroptimist, etc.)

Chamber of Commerce

PTA

Hospital volunteer auxiliary

Environmental society

Political parties or action groups

Art association

Concert or theater ushers

Friends of the local public garden

Museum docents

Adult leaders of scouts, Y, boys & girls clubs

Youth soccer, Little League, gymnastics, volleyball

Meals on Wheels

Historical society

Food bank

Hotline crisis telephone service

League of Women Voters

Church World Service

Beta Sigma Phi

Hadassah

American Association of University Women

Red Cross

United Way

Check it out. There's a group out there that needs you!

Don't just "join up" however. Let your involvement be an avenue for new friendships, and new ways to explore yourself. However, if you become an active "committee woman," you may find yourself taking on an additional layer of stress too quickly ("can you get that done by Friday?"), instead of gaining friends and expanding your social horizons. As you put your toe into the water of a social group, look for *people relationships,* not for extra jobs to do. Sure, you'll be asked to help, and you'll want to carry your share of whatever the group is up to, but don't let that be your main focus, at least not for now. You're looking for ways to build your own life, not to single-handedly create the most dynamic service group in town. Contribute your talents generously, but don't give your life away.

Make Music

Somewhere, sometime, probably way back in school, you played a musical instrument. In fact, you may have a tarnished old flute or trumpet or an aging viola in the back of a closet or in your rented storage unit. How long since you've played? Ten years? Fifteen?

Okay, now that your secret is out, what say you dig out the old axe and play a few bars — or even just a few notes? See there — you can still do it! No excuses now. Find out what's happening on the local amateur music scene. Hundreds of towns across the country have community bands and other ensembles, and many are geared for folks who haven't touched their horns or strings in years.

Playing in a musical group — at whatever level fits your talent — can be rewarding in many ways, not the least of which is that you'll be out of the house and meeting people with a common interest.

Play Ball!

But wait! We're not yet finished with the groups you can join to get yourself out in the mainstream. Joining a gym can have the added benefit of "narrowing your posterior" while it broadens your horizons. But what about a sports group of some sort? Many communities have organized or loosely organized sports groups for adults, which may be under the auspices of an organization — such as the Y or a religious congregation or the local public schools — or may be more of an "ad hoc" type of thing. Your community may have public tennis courts, handball courts, basketball courts, and/or volleyball courts at which you can organize a game or join one in progress, whether it's all-women or co-ed. Many golf clubs also have tennis courts, racquetball courts, swimming pools, and other sports facilities.

Check your local newspaper, too. Cynthia MacGregor was at one time a member of an informal volleyball group that met every Sunday in a county park. The group was designed for singles over thirty-five. The woman who had formed the group was tired of playing in pick-up volleyball games in which she was the only person over twenty and therefore the weakest player, and/or the only person who wasn't half of a couple. So she formed her own group and advertised it in the newspaper, specifying it was for singles over thirty-five.

As the group became more cohesive, the members began having Sunday evening dinners together in different inexpensive restaurants and Sunday night games nights at which members played card games, board games, and backgammon. Though no long-term romances ensued among the members of the group, some brief alliances resulted, and several long-term friendships were forged. As well, the members got some great exercise playing volleyball, tried out some new restaurants, had some great fun on game nights, and learned some new game skills.

New Directions?

Learning something new is rewarding. Whether you're seeking a course, a club, a volunteer opportunity, or a religious congregation, don't look only for one that focuses on your long-time enjoyments. Be bold and try something new! This chapter is about broadening your horizons, and we want to point out that, while it's good to meet new people while also learning more about your long-time hobby — photography, cooking, quilting, genealogy, backpacking — it's at least as good if not better to strike out boldly toward new interests. Join a cultural club in which you can meet new people, learn a new language, learn the customs and proverbs and native dances of Portugal and Brazil, and learn to eat and cook Brazilian and Portuguese cuisine. (Or whatever culture and cuisine might interest you, be it Mexican, Italian, Ethiopian, Russian, Arabic, Japanese....)

And while we're talking about getting multiple benefits out of joining a group, how about joining a singles group that focuses on personal growth, or that offers discussion groups about the travails of being divorced, or about the situations specific to being a single parent? Now you're not only expanding your horizons by meeting new people but are also growing as a person and interacting with others who face the same challenges you do and can perhaps offer coping suggestions.

Naturally, of course, the friends you meet in whatever activities you pursue can offer coping suggestions outside the structure of the group as well. Part of the whole point of getting out and meeting new people is to meet people in similar circumstances to yours. Your old married friends, no matter how close you are to them, can sympathize with the situations you encounter in your new, divorced state, but they're less likely to be able to give you solid advice. They *might* be able to give you good common-sense suggestions. They might even have other divorced friends who are dealing with the same situations you are. But they haven't "been there, done that" themselves.

The new single friends you meet, on the other hand, and especially the divorced ones, are facing many of the same situations you are. If your mother keeps urging you to return to your abusive husband, or your son is angry and sullen because "you made Daddy leave; it's all your fault," or your male associate at work treats you totally differently now that he assumes you're an "available" divorcée, or there are nights you're scared and lonely and wonder if you ought to beg your ex to take you back, these are situations your new, divorced friends can speak to from experience. Maybe not every one of them has dealt with all the same issues you're experiencing, but collectively, they'll have great suggestions for many of the challenges you now face.

This is another reason to expand the horizons of your life to include new friends. You aren't just trying to enlarge your window of experiences. You're building a personal support system.

Becoming Independent

No doubt about it, there have been major life changes for you recently. You were a wife, part of a partnership, member of a team, half of a couple. Now you're on your own. Without a partner. A single woman. Alone. Independent...or are you?

Maybe you've never been on your own before. It's not unusual to go from home to school to college to marriage without living alone. Now you have to learn how to "make it" in the world as a single person, maybe as a single parent, too.

Being independent is more than being alone. Independence is an earned quality. It requires courage, stamina, knowledge, judgment, decision-making, self-expression, a level of financial security and, paradoxically, a solid support system.

Courage. "It isn't easy bein' green," Kermit tells us. "Green," as the felt frog views it, is a euphemism for "different." And to be an independent woman in our society, despite the gains in women's rights over the past century, is still to be different. We've talked about all the well-meaning friends and relatives who want to know about your latest male friend, or when you'll be getting married again. And what about this career of yours? Surely you don't expect to find a new husband by assertively working your way up the ladder of management!

Yes, it does require a good deal of courage -- and more than a little self-assurance -- to forge an independent life for yourself. Courage to challenge others' assumptions about what's right for you. Courage to raise your children alone. Courage to confront those who would manipulate you on the job, in the marketplace, in the community.

Stamina. Oh yeah! It's well known that women are much more capable at multi-tasking than men. Men work an eight-hour day and come home exhausted, expecting to relax. Women have been working dawn to bedtime for centuries. It's stamina you have, unless you have serious illness. And it's stamina you'll need if you're to balance work, home management, children, finances, career advancement, dealing with your ex, new relationships, and so much more on your own.

Judgment and decision-making. "The rubber," as they say, "meets the road" about here. As you go about handling all the myriad challenges of living independently, you're confronted with hundreds of decisions, small and large, personal and professional, private and parental, that require sound judgment. You've got to know how and where to get the facts, how to assess them, who to trust for advice, when it's time to hold 'em and when to fold 'em. Most often, circumstances and other people will conspire to rush you to a decision. "If you buy it today, I'll throw in a year's supply of detergent." And just as often, your long-term best interests are served by not allowing yourself to be rushed. Get the facts you need, get second opinions, do a little online or library research, consider both short-term and long-term consequences for yourself and others involved, weigh the pros and cons. You may miss a few opportunities by taking time to reach solid conclusions, but you'll find the payoffs for careful consideration will outweigh any benefits of a quick decision in the vast majority of situations.

Assertiveness and self-expression. The term "assertiveness" scares a lot of people. Too many equate it with "aggressiveness," and view it as pushy, rude. Not so. Dr. Bob has been teaching and writing about assertiveness for over thirty years; be assured that it's a positive, healthy style of action that will benefit you and those around you. The idea is to express yourself without being pushy, and with respect for others. Too many women have been socialized to hold back their opinions, to discount their own value, to behave as if they don't deserve to be recognized or counted. To be assertive is simply to claim your perfect right to an equal playing field. You have as much inherent value as any other human being — your ex, your current squeeze, your attorney, your physician, your landlord, the judge — and no one has a right to push you around or make you do things their way — well, maybe the judge. If you've been used to being at the bottom of the heap when it comes to whose opinions and ideas matter, it's time to develop some assertive skills and let yourself be heard. Dr. Bob's book, *Your Perfect Right: Assertiveness and Equality in Your Life and Relationships,* is a good place to start.

Financial security. This one is tough, because if you don't have it, it isn't easy to get it. A good education is an invaluable start, along with a career, a solid job with a stable company, some savings, a retirement plan, your own home, few if any debts. All are measures of financial security but can be hard to come by if you are in debt, on your own, have little or no college, no strong career prospects, and/or pay month-to-month rent. Unfortunately, our society is not necessarily geared to helping those who need it the most. We also tend to encourage folks to live beyond their means, buying all the latest gadgets, designer children's wear, unneeded sports equipment, and as new and nice a car as one can possibly afford. Autos are sold with five- or six-year loans, insuring that the buyer will always owe more than the car is worth. Children are bombarded with advertising and peer pressure that burdens parents with the old "but ALL the kids have them!" whine. It takes a courageous and far-sighted mom to withstand these forces and keep her eye on the future well-being of herself and her family.

The more you know... Although it won't contribute much to your social life, an online course may enhance your career, expand your interests, enrich a hobby, prepare you for a leadership role in a community organization, or perhaps just help you keep track of your financial situation.

Getting involved. We've covered this one pretty well earlier in the chapter. Suffice here to say that your community needs you, and you need your community.

Building a personal support system. A community organization may not be your best path to the support system you need. Maybe you're not that interested in groups, and you'd be happier playing bunko at home, meeting a few friends for coffee, or talking with another mom at the park a couple of days a week.

What we're suggesting here is that you find ways — ways that fit you and your lifestyle — to connect with others who can offer emotional support. Whether it's your extended family — mom, sisters, aunts, cousins — or your neighbors, your old friends from school, or maybe a singles group that focuses on personal growth, you're looking for a very few folks you can rely on to be there when you need to talk to someone, ask for a ride when your car's in the shop, swap a couple of hours of childcare, get advice on that job offer, find a new ob/gyn, or just to get that baby food stain out of the carpet.

Friends like that are precious, not easily found, and worthy of care and nurturing. When you have them, give more than you get, be there when they need you, and make that relationship a high priority in your life.

Consider yourself extremely fortunate if you have caring parents, siblings, friends, co-workers, neighbors, interest group members, and others to whom you can turn when you need advice, support, a shoulder to cry on, even a short-term loan. We all need the love and support of others. If you're not getting your share, it's time to go to work at developing those precious relationships among people who can be there when you need them. Whose ear is there when you really need someone to talk with? Whose arm is strong enough — and patient enough — to carry you through a crisis? Who do you ask for recommendations when your car or your dog or your refrigerator — or your child — needs repair? The phone book is a fine resource for looking up numbers, but not a particularly trustworthy source of advice for selecting a professional. If, on the other hand, you have a network of people to whom you can address such questions, you'll be light years ahead in getting the help you need when the time comes to find solace, advice, medical help, an attorney, a mechanic, or a plumber.

Making the Most of New Activities

As you consider the ideas in this chapter for broadening your horizons, keep in mind that we're not suggesting you seek change just for change's sake. It can be a temptation to seek just *any* change when your life is in a state of flux and transition. Whether you sought the divorce or your ex did, you're probably feeling unsettled right now. You may already be looking ahead toward your next relationship or feel that you're done with men and marriage. (At least, that's how you feel *now*.) But either way, you're probably restless. You want things to get better, your life to get back on an even track, your future to look brighter, your finances to become easier to deal with. You'd like a lot of things to be different.

Things *will* get better. Reach out sensibly to new possibilities as you create the good life for yourself and your children. Seek opportunities for growth or improvement.

Broaden your horizons. Better days are ahead!

AfterWords — Chapter Five

Key Points in the Chapter

- Life changes around your divorce may offer opportunities for expanding your world.

- You might choose to go back to school, finish college, get an advanced degree, gain special career skills, or just learn more about the world around you.

- There are many places in your own community to meet new people and make new friends, including neighborhood, school, clubs, religious congregations, musical groups, sports teams, and any of the volunteer organizations doing community service.

- As you connect with new people in your life, look for ways to make each new relationship a chance for growth toward a better life on your own.

- Becoming an independent person means developing courage, stamina, judgment, decision-making skills, assertiveness, financial security, involvement, and a strong personal support system.

Activity of the Week

- If you're not already involved in volunteer community activities, attend at least one meeting this week of a volunteer organization you haven't been to before.

- If you're an active volunteer already, look around at your next meeting, and introduce yourself to two people you've not met before.

- Spend some time with your journal, making notes about what you gain from volunteering, and how you could expand the personal benefits of those activities. (We're not suggesting you get "selfish" about it; just consider the value to yourself.)

Suggested Readings and Resources

Alberti, R.E. & Emmons, M.L. (2001). *Your Perfect Right: Assertiveness and Equality in Your Life and Relationships* (eighth edition). Atascadero, CA: Impact Publishers.

Covey, S.R. (1990). *Seven Habits of Highly Effective People: Powerful Lessons in Personal Change.* New York: Fireside/Simon & Schuster.

Phelps, S. & Austin, N. (2002). *The Assertive Woman* (fourth edition). Atascadero, CA: Impact Publishers.

After Your Divorce

PART TWO

"Stuff" in Your Life

6

· · · · · · · · · ·

Practical Matters

"**T**WO CAN LIVE AS CHEAPLY AS ONE**," goes an old myth that launched a lot of marriages — not always successfully. True or not (not likely!), it's not even cheap for one any more, especially if you can't do a lot of everyday "stuff" for yourself. There are bound to be times when you miss having a husband.

It may be something as simple as needing help around the house with one of those chores he used to do. It may be that you need to get ten-year-old Roger to band practice at the same time twelve-year-old Courtney pitches her first softball game or plays in the all-city championships. When you were married, one parent could chauffeur Roger while the other went to Courtney's game. What are you going to do now?

You probably didn't realize, until a while after the divorce, how long was your list of things that depended on his help. If your husband was a traditional handyman-about-the-house, you may have relied on him for repairs. If he was appreciably taller than you, he was there for reaching things in high places. And maybe it was he who kept the cars running and the lawnmower humming.

When you run out of milk unexpectedly, do you have to get the kids dressed and take them out with you on an emergency milk run because they're too young to stay alone and there's no one to go to the store for you? When you have to do a full-scale grocery-shopping run, do you have to bring three kids with you (and take twice as long to get through the store) because there's no one to stay home with them while you go shopping? Your teenagers may be old enough to stay by themselves when you have to work late, but can they fix dinner?

Maybe your husband wasn't the handyman type but was the family chef. Or one of those rare guys who are surprisingly good with the sewing machine, letting down hems, fixing rips, and re-sewing buttons on the family's clothes. Maybe he couldn't unclog a toilet, but was a whiz at balancing the checkbook. Did he build spice racks and bookcases and toy chests?

Maybe he gave you backrubs whenever your back was achy. Maybe he did all the night driving because you didn't feel comfortable driving in the dark, even with your new glasses. Maybe he was your intrepid bug-killer, or your go-to guy when the question was, "What was that noise?"

Who's going to do all that now?

Good Help Is Hard to Find

Your first step is to accept that all these jobs still have to be done, and now they're yours to do. This chapter offers a laundry list of practical steps you can take to deal with some of these everyday matters that used to go on your "honey-do" list. We trust you'll find a few tips that will work for you.

All Those Handy"man" Jobs

❖ For anything around the house in the way of handyman work or similar, you can hire a paid handyman.

❖ Many communities have appliance service businesses that, for a fixed annual fee, will make as many "house calls" as needed to fix major appliances (often plumbing is included or can be added to the contract).

❖ If you have a handy friend or relative, male or female, or a female friend with a handy husband, you may be able to lean on this person when needed, as long as you make it plain that you'll accept the help only if they'll allow you to trade favors. The payback can be in the form of home-cooked meals that you invite your handyman friend (and his or her family) over for, or frozen home-cooked main courses that you send home with him or her, or services offered in trade, whether you sew, tutor a child, groom a dog, manicure nails, or provide some other needed service.

❖ We will discuss, in chapter 12, some of the ins and outs of relying on your ex and offering him appropriate paybacks in return.

❖ You can trade with another single mom or dad, doing things for each other, whether it's snaking a slow-running sink or picking up a child from a birthday party.

Jill and Heather are neighbors. Though they always were cordial to each other when they ran into each other, they never were friends, never socialized. Heather doesn't work. Her husband travels frequently on business. Her kids are older than Jill's, so they never hung out with Heather's kids. Jill, a busy graphics designer, had gone back to work right after the birth of each of her kids. She and her husband and kids were a tight little family unit...till her husband dropped a bombshell and told her he wanted a divorce.

When Jill's husband left her, word got around the condo complex, and Heather rang the door with a sympathetic, "If I can help in any way...." At first Jill sloughed it off, but when Heather repeated, "I mean it. I'm not just saying it. You're going to need practical help. Trust me. I'm alone with the kids often enough. I know," Jill processed the offer mentally and made a note to remember.

The occasion to need help came soon enough. It was something really silly: a jar that wouldn't open no matter what tricks Jill tried. Formerly, she would have presented the jar to her husband. Now he wasn't around. Sheepishly she rang Heather's bell. Heather inserted a can opener point under the lid, broke the vacuum seal, and opened the jar. Jill was duly impressed.

Two nights later, a history homework assignment that had buffaloed Jill's son (and Jill herself) sent her reluctantly to Heather's door again. "Don't sweat it," Heather laughed when Jill apologized, "I may need some help myself. My daughter has geometry this year, and math's not my strong suit."

"I can help!" Jill eagerly replied. "I was a math whiz in school."

Heather helped Jill's son with his homework while Jill helped Heather's daughter.

"Why don't you let me fix dinner for you tomorrow night?" Heather suggested. "I'm home all day, you know."

"I couldn't let you. That would be taking advantage."

"You could and you will. And I'll take advantage right back. I need someone to drive Barry to a party on Saturday just at the hour I have to be on the other side of town dropping Melinda at another party."

"Jill's chauffeuring service," the newly divorced woman quipped.

"I bet you have a list of chores that need to be done around the house," Heather offered. "I'm pretty good at handyman stuff myself. A regular Pauline the Plumber. But anything that's beyond me, my husband can handle. He'll be home next Wednesday…for a week, till he leaves again," she sighed. "Give me your list."

"I don't have one yet," Jill answered. "Honestly. But I know whose doorbell to ring now when something needs fixing."

Jill and Heather never did become close friends, but they formed a mutual help alliance that benefited both of them.

Feeding Time

What about cooking? How do you handle that if you're back at work full-time since the divorce, or if your husband used to help with the cooking — or maybe did all of it — and now is no longer around? Whether you're feeding kids or just yourself, you don't want to eat take-out every night. And store-bought frozen foods are both pricey and unsatisfying. If you're a big fan of Julia Child or Jacques Pepin, you can skip this section, but if you could use a boost in the kitchen, any one or more of the following solutions might help:

❖ Trade dinners with a friend. She can cook for you some nights while you cook for her other nights. (Or you can do her some other favor instead of cooking.) This cooking for each other can (but doesn't need to) involve eating at each other's house. You might be able to stop at her house on your way home from work, pick up dinner packaged "to go," and take it home. But especially if you're both singles with no kids, a little company at dinner might be nice.

❖ Buy a slow cooker (often referred to by a popular brand name, "Crockpot™") if you don't have one already. There are many dishes you can prepare in the morning, leave cooking slowly in the slow cooker all day, and eat when you get home. In many cases they are all-in-one meals, including meat, potatoes, and veggies. A complete dinner is ready for you when you get home from work — or as soon thereafter as you're ready for it. If the recipe is not one that includes potatoes and veggies, you can make a simple potato, vegetable, or tossed salad to go with the meat.

❖ Cook large quantities of main courses on the weekend, freeze what you cook in single servings, and defrost as needed during the week. If you're eating alone, defrost just one serving. If you bring a friend home from work, defrost two servings. If your two kids each have a friend over, defrost five servings. You can cook double recipes and have a freezer full of ready-to-defrost meals. Keep fresh salad greens on hand. For more variety, on alternate days mix in occasional take-out, or barbeque some chicken breasts. Kids love "breakfast for dinner." Whip up some eggs, bacon, and a bowl of fruit. You'll be way ahead when the kids ask, "What's for dinner?"

❖ Plan for leftovers. Cook a large quantity of something simple, like baked or roasted chicken, hamburgers (turkeyburgers, veggie burgers), or a pork roast. The next night (or the night after that), do something creative but relatively easy with the leftovers: the chicken becomes chicken à la king or chicken salad; the burgers are converted to chili or a pasta dish; the pork is chunked and cooked up with frozen corn, diced green peppers and onions, seasoned to taste with a little wine and served over instant rice.

❖ Teach your older kids some kitchen skills. Don't expect them to fix dinner this week, but get them started on learning the basics. They can start by helping you plan a meal, get the ingredients together, dig packages out of the freezer to thaw, grease a muffin pan. Washing and tearing the lettuce for salad is a child-friendly job. Before long, they'll be old enough to learn simple knife chores — such as cutting up the fresh vegetables — under your supervision. (Teach safety first or you may be spending the dinner hour at the emergency room!) As they grow — and after a lesson or two in hot stove safety — they can cook canned soup, or boil the water for hot cereal. In time, and with your help, they'll be fixing simple dishes on their own, maybe making packaged brownies or muffins or cooking sausages or steaming the veggies. Probably before you know it, they'll have dinner ready when you get home from work! Well...maybe not this month, but maybe sooner than you expect. The key to this process is patience, allowing them to make mistakes, and keeping your cool — and sense of humor — when they blow it. The rewards — for both of you — will be enormous. You'll have help in the kitchen, and they'll be developing skills and a sense of responsibility that will last all their lives.

Kids and School

Most of what we have to say about your children appears in other chapters. But one "practical" aspect of parenting that belongs here is your relationship to the schools that educate your kids.

Use your own good judgment as a parent. Don't depend on what other parents are doing, but find out what they're doing. Get to know the teachers. Go to your kids' events. Keep them balanced between homework, school, and activities. They don't have to fill every minute, but if they have lots of time for Nintendo or TV, they need other activities. "Adding up TV and computer time, two- to seventeen-year-olds spend an average of four and a half hours a day in front of electronic screens at home," says psychotherapist Dr. Peter Fraenkel. (One can only wonder how many hours are added by PlayStations, Nintendo, and similar games!) Get 'em outside and involved in physical activities!

Don't get uptight about all the standardized tests thrown at the kids at school — and help the kids to relax about them too. The tests have become a bureaucratic substitute for knowing what kids are really learning. The major tests offer politicians a way to say how schools are doing — compared to other schools. They do not measure the truly important things kids need to learn: real-world problem-solving skills, getting along with others, taking responsibility for themselves, learning how to learn (and loving it), the joy of reading, wanting to go beyond the minimum requirements and really find out about a subject. The sad fact is, teachers must now focus their attention on preparing kids for the tests, not for life.

Money and Other Matters

Did you handle the checkbook when you were married? Arrange for home maintenance and repairs? Negotiate for cars and credit? Manage your family's investments? If so, you may choose to skip this section.

Since lots of divorced women find themselves dealing with these mundane but often challenging life issues alone for the first time, we've summarized here a few tips to make that transition a bit easier. There are no quick and easy solutions to such major concerns as family finances or auto maintenance. What you will find here are some tried and true resources that will help you learn how to handle those troublesome financial issues more effectively.

Credit. If you don't already have it, get credit *in your own name* as soon as you can. But use it carefully — only when you really need it. (Remember, *credit cards are your most expensive debt*). If you're starting out, buy a few items on your card(s), but only what you can pay off at the end of the month. That will help to build a favorable credit history.

❖ Use your credit cards wisely. If you already have debts, whenever you get a few dollars ahead, pay off any credit card debt first. Cards charge the most in interest — up to 20%, compared to around 6% for a home mortgage, even less for a car loan. If possible, charge only what you can pay off in 30 days

❖ Don't finance a car for five years or more — you'll always owe more than it's worth and be in trouble if you have to sell it prematurely. If you can't afford the payments for a three-year loan, you probably can't afford that car. Best of all: keep the old heap going as long as it's safe, and save to pay cash — or a major down payment — for the next one. Cars are not like computers, they don't double in speed and power every year, so you may not need a new one as soon as you think.

Personal Finance. Save, save, save. Divorce recovery time is belt-tightening time. Whatever your financial situation before the divorce, unless you were very wealthy and walked away with a major share of that wealth, chances are you're living on a lot less now. Keep it in mind as you budget and spend.

❖ Buy life insurance only if you have dependents, and buy only term insurance. "Cash value" is a myth. Invest the difference in your kids' education or paying off your debts.

❖ Be wary of advisors who sell products (such as "financial planners" who sell stocks or mutual funds). Pay for services and get independent advice.

❖ Max out your IRA and 401K — think long range. It may squeeze you now, but you'll be very glad later! Fund a Roth IRA to minimize the tax bite.

❖ Teach your kids how to handle money from an early age — and teach your daughter the same things you teach your son.

❖ A recent article in *Money* magazine suggested that you're a "financial grown-up" when you realize that (1) the right time to save is always now (not "when you finish..."), (2) the only one you can count on is you (not your parents, your boss, your ex...), (3) you are your own best financial adviser (get advice, but don't follow blindly), (4) you'll screw up sometimes (you're human like the rest of us), (5) less is really more (it's not what you have that counts, it's what you need).

❖ If you have more than a few dollars in the bank, get a CPA and discuss your financial situation. Don't wait for April 15 to ask for professional help getting your financial life in order.

❖ Watch out for investment fees. Invest where fees are low. Buy no-load mutual funds. Look for minimum charges on IRA accounts. Check out low-cost funds at Vanguard, Fidelity, T. Rowe Price. Avoid funds that charge more than 1% in fees, or funds with "loads" (12b, or purchase or redemption fees). Don't "churn" your investments — the more often you buy and sell, the bigger the tax bite.

❖ Be sure your will is up to date; things have changed, big time, as a result of the divorce.

❖ Have you changed the beneficiaries on your insurance policies, IRAs, 401K, bank account(s), and other investments? You probably do not want him to be the target of your generosity! Don't put this off. Go through the list and be sure you've notified every company and institution you deal with. Check with your attorney to be sure the proper documents have been filed so your ex cannot incur debt in your name. And be sure all your credit accounts — credit card companies, banks, department stores, utilities, oil & gas companies, online stores, whatever — are formally notified that you're not responsible for his debts. You may have already cut up the cards, but you need to notify the companies in writing as well.

❖ Consider joining a local credit union. These excellent financial institutions are like a bank that's owned by the customers. Loan rates are the best you'll find. They often pay interest on checking funds. And they're usually the most user-friendly banks around.

❖ If you were not handling the family finances when you were married, take a class on personal financial management. Or at least read a couple of books on the subject. (See the Resources list at the end of the chapter.) It's not brain surgery, but there are some things you need to know.

❖ Watch your back. Keep your records private. So-called "identity theft" is reported to be the fastest-growing form of crime today, and you do not want to be a victim. Shred unneeded documents. Use credit cards only when necessary. Use only secure sites for online shopping. Don't give out your social security number unless it is absolutely necessary (ask if an alternate form of identification will suffice).

Information Resources. Remember libraries? They're still the best information resources around, even in the age of Google and Yahoo and Ask Jeeves. Check out used book stores, too.

❖ Expand your media coverage beyond the major commercial networks — ABC, CBS, CNN, NBC — which tend to offer watered down, mainstream, "press release" news. Be especially wary of sources that tout only one viewpoint, such as talk radio and Fox News. Check out NPR, PBS, Discovery.... Rely on multiple sources. Look for facts, not hype. Those who have all the answers probably aren't asking the right questions.

❖ Vote.

Taking Care of Your Home. Owning your own home is almost always your best investment. ("Almost" because there are communities where home values go down, but that's the exception.) Keep it if you possibly can! Of course, *owning* means *caring for,* and that means time and money and some expertise.

❖ Get a couple of home maintenance books (again, see the Resources list at the end of the chapter) so you can do simple jobs yourself. Ask lots of questions at your favorite hardware store (get a favorite hardware store!), including their recommendations for local fix-it folks. Take a fix-it-yourself class at the local community college or adult education school, or at that favorite hardware store.

❖ Seek online resources for all kinds of practical health, home, and financial questions, but evaluate sources carefully! Look for ideas and themes that come up often. Remember that lots of what you find will be promoting particular products. Use computers at the library if you don't have one available at home.

We Never Said It Was Going to Be Easy!

The suggestions we've offered in this chapter cover a lot of territory. Much of this material may not apply to you. That's okay; if just one or two ideas fit your situation, we've done our jobs. And none of this stuff is carved in stone. You'll have your own ways of dealing with these practical issues, and many of them will be better than ours. What we hope to do here is to help you feel empowered to go on alone. You can handle these everyday matters that are now yours to manage on your own. Check out the Resources section at the end of each caption for reading material on topics that interest you. We've suggested a few books and web sites that we think will help if you want to pursue a subject further.

You can do this!

AfterWords — Chapter Six

Key Points in the Chapter

- Lots of everyday activities are easier with two. You'll notice his absence, even if you used to wind up at each other's throat.

- You may need to hire help for some of the "handyman" jobs he used to do, but you'll find you can do many of them yourself.

- He was the family chef? No matter. You can fix healthy and satisfying meals with a little planning and preparation. You won't be Julia Child on your first try, but you can do this.

- Err on the conservative side in your financial affairs. Save a little every month.

- Use credit wisely, and only when necessary. Don't overextend yourself. Save and pay cash instead.

- Caring for your home, car, appliances, etc., will be less costly — and less hassle — in the long run than fixing them when they break. Keep up with regular maintenance.

Activity of the Week

- Inventory time! Take out your journal and walk through your home, jotting down an inventory of all your valuables, furniture, etc. For each item, make a quick estimate of its value, condition, and if it needs service or other attention. Draft an action plan for taking care of what needs to be done. Make some calls — or visit the hardware store — to get the ball rolling.

Suggested Readings and Resources

Finance

Bottom Line/Personal newsletter — www.bottomlinesecrets.com

Quinn, J.B. (1997). *Making the Most of Your Money.* New York: Simon and Schuster.

Tyson, E. (2003). *Personal Finance for Dummies* (fourth edition). New York: For Dummies Books/Wiley.

Fix-It Yourself

Carey, J. (2000). *Home Maintenance for Dummies.* New York: For Dummies Books/Wiley.

Sussman, J., and Glakas-Tenet, S. (2002). *Dare to Repair.* New York: HarperResource 2002

Reader's Digest (2004). *Reader's Digest Complete Do-It-Yourself Manual.* Pleasantville, NY: Reader's Digest Press.

After Your Divorce

PART THREE

Kids in Your Life

7

•••••••••

"What Have I Done to My Kids?"

ALL TOO OFTEN DIVORCE WILL CAUSE a woman to feel that she has done a disservice to her children — especially if she was the one who asked for the divorce.

If you lose your temper easily with your kids, for instance, you may feel you're caught in another post-divorce pit: the "what-have-I-done-to-my-kids" guilt factor. They lived in a two-parent home till you asked for the divorce. Now Daddy doesn't live here anymore, he isn't around to play catch with Jenny or help Ryan with his algebra homework or do all the other "Daddy things" that the kids used to enjoy and rely on...and it's all *your* fault.

Not!

First of all, you asked for the divorce *for a reason.* It wasn't a whim. It wasn't done on a lark. In all probability you didn't just "fall out of love." Something your ex did (or failed to do) triggered your unhappiness with the marriage and caused you to ask for a divorce. So it's hardly "all your fault" that your kids no longer have their dad living with them.

And second, if the atmosphere in the house was tense, or a good deal of fighting was going on, or you two hardly spoke to each other at all, this was *not* a good thing for the kids. Living in a battle-free zone with one parent is definitely the lesser of the two evils. Not only is it unhealthy for them to live in conditions of turmoil but, had you remained in such a marriage, you'd have been modeling that constant fighting or bickering or taking nasty jabs at each other is an acceptable way to live. That an atmosphere of cold silence is an acceptable way to relate. If your husband was emotionally, verbally, or physically abusive, and you took it, you were modeling a lack of self-respect. That doesn't help kids grow into adults who are able to form firm and healthy relationships of their own.

Believe it or not, you've done a good thing for your kids by divorcing their father!

S'Mothering and Spoiling

Here is an appropriate time to insert a word or two about a very common error. Too many parents (usually moms) try to compensate for their kids' "deprivation" of the absent parent, or for what the mom has "done to" the kids by divorcing the dad...and they go about it in all the wrong ways. An absent father is guilty of a similar misdeed to the one we're focusing on here. (They have their own way of overcompensating. We'll talk about "the Ice-Cream Man" and "Disneyland Dad" in chapter 7.) But right now, we're talking about the *primary residential parent* — most frequently the mom — and what she does to the kids in the name of "making it up to them."

What does she do? Most often, and most serious, she *spoils* them. Less often, less serious, but still wrong, she emotionally *smothers* them. There are at least two different root causes of emotional smothering, and both are wrong. Let's talk about spoiling first.

Driven by guilt, the mother may buy her kids whatever they ask for...maybe not literally everything they demand, but certainly far too much of it. Ignoring budgetary realities and the fact that it isn't emotionally healthy for kids to get everything they ask for, the "guilty" mother will buy them toys, games, clothes, fancy sneakers, and more. She'll take them to the mall, their favorite fast food restaurant, or a nearby amusement park.

Mama Softouch will acquiesce to unreasonable demands on not just her money but her time, acting as an on-call chauffeur, when what she really needs is to stay home and chill out, when the kids should stay home and clean their rooms, or when the kids could ride their bikes, take the bus, or even walk! She'll let them off the hook on room-cleaning and other chores. Really little ones who always got one bedtime story now demand and get three. And if they howl for a later bedtime, Mom will let them stay up. "They've had it rough lately," she says to herself. "I'm just making it up to them. Their father is gone" ("It's all my fault," she'll add, if she was the one who asked for the divorce.) "If I can make it up to them in any way, let me do it."

Besides "making it up to them" — giving in to their many demands for toys, ice cream and junk food, special privileges, special outings or being driven here, there, and everywhere, and for being excused from chores and tasks and other obligations — there is another way some moms try to compensate for the dad's absence: They try to give the kids extra time and loving themselves.

In theory, it sounds great: "Their dad is around only for weekend visits. Let me make sure the kids get enough attention, and enough time, from me." What could be wrong with that? Nothing at all...in moderation. In moderation, it's a great idea.

But some moms lavish so much affection and so much attention on their kids that they smother them emotionally. From a never-ending torrent of "How was your day?"-type questions to an unwarranted (and unwanted) amount of hugging and kissing, to making conversation when the child would rather be talking on the phone with a friend, reading a book, playing a video game, or out bike-riding. These moms overdo it by a mile.

There is another cause, besides guilt, that sometimes drives divorced moms to engage in excessive, unwanted conversations with their kids: the absence of another adult in the house to talk to. Too often, with no husband to talk with anymore, Mom tries to make a friend out of one or more of her kids — especially if she has a "tween" or teen daughter — and tries to use this child to fill up the empty space in her life. *Don't.* Make adult friends. Your children need to be children. They're not ready emotionally for the responsibility of being your peers!

Time's Up!

Now here's another loop on the emotional roller coaster: your feelings about spending time with your kids. As a good parent, you would spend some time every day with them under any circumstances. *How much* time depends on a variety of factors, including their ages (at three or five they need more of your time than they do at eleven, and at fifteen they may be actively avoiding spending much time with you) and what other events and needs are laying claim to your time. If you work, if you have four or five kids, or if you are helping care for an elderly parent or ill sibling, to cite some examples, you will certainly have less time to spend with each of your kids. Assuming the divorce has left you with residential custody of one or more minor children, you probably want to spend even more time with your kids than you did before. Yet you may now have *less* available time to spend.

While you know you can't literally be both Mom and Dad to them (hopefully Dad is still in the picture, even though no longer in the home), you feel an understandable wish to give more of yourself to help make up for what they miss by his not being there. Too, if they're crying, acting out, verbally expressing regret that Daddy's gone, or otherwise giving indications that the divorce has impacted them, you want to help them get over the hurdle. You attempt to do this by spending extra time with them, listening to their concerns, soothing their tears and fears, keeping them occupied with more pleasant things, and trying to show them that, even though Daddy's gone, much of the rest of their lives is still as it was before, including your very definite presence.

On the other hand...

❖ The more they act out and are impossible to be with, the less time you *want* to spend with them, even though you know they need you. Intellectually you know they're being bratty because they're in emotional pain, but that doesn't make them any more pleasant to be with.

❖ You have some very real claims on your time, more than ever before, that are pulling you in other directions. Perhaps you didn't work until the divorce, and now you need to hold down a job in order to keep food on the table. Or perhaps you worked only part-time and now are working full-time. You may even be working a second job now, or doing some type of work from home in the evenings, to make ends meet. Maybe you've gone back to school to advance your career. You have more to do around the house, too. Whether your husband helped a lot around the house or just a little, now that he's gone, whatever tasks he shouldered fall squarely on you now. Did he used to feed the baby while you cooked dinner for the rest of the family? Did he help with the laundry? Take out the trash, water the lawn, pull the weeds, wash the car, help run errands? Or simply keep the three-year-old safely busy while you helped the nine-year-old with his homework? Whatever he did, he's not there doing it now, and so it all falls to you... and minimizes the time you have available to spend with the kids.

❖ Last, but far from least, *you need time for yourself.* You need to regroup emotionally, "catch your breath," vent to your friends and/or family, read a book or write in your diary, lose your troubles in a good rented movie, or go putter among your houseplants — whatever you find that's therapeutic for you.

Now, we can't and won't tell you *how* to budget your time, but we do want to urge you to understand two things:

❖ *You are only one person.* You are not Superwoman, and it won't accomplish anything to berate yourself if you can't do all the things you'd like to.

❖ *There are only twenty-four hours in a day.* You cannot change that fact. If the house doesn't get vacuumed as often as it used to, as long as it's not so dirty that it's unhealthy, don't fret about it. If dinner isn't served at 6:00 on the dot any longer, or if you serve frozen green peas three days a week because they're the easiest vegetable to prepare, or if it's hamburgers instead of meatloaf because they're quicker, don't beat yourself up over it. And if you don't spend as much time with the kids as you think you ought to, as long as you're not neglecting them, and you respond when they really need you, then you are "there" for them.

If You Don't Take Care of Yourself...

The kids *are* going to go through some pain on account of the divorce. It's inevitable. *And it's not your fault.* You can help them up to a point. You cannot erase the difficulty completely, not even if you were to spend twenty-four/seven with them (which wouldn't be healthy — for them or for you!), so don't feel you need to spend every waking moment with them, or feel guilty that you can't.

❖ You need to take care of your own emotional needs, not only for your own sake but for your children's. By taking time to soothe your own emotions and salve your own wounds you are not only helping yourself to heal and cope, but making yourself stronger so you can better help your kids. If you fall apart, break down in tears, or fly off the handle on minimal provocation, find yourself unable to make decisions, deal with crises, shoulder the day-to-day burdens, or have the emotional fortitude to put up with an angry teenager, a rebellious three-year-old, or an emotional eleven-year-old, you will not be able to provide the help and the emotional stability that your kids need — now more than ever.

So take the time to do what you need to do for yourself, for your own emotional well-being, for your own stability. And don't begrudge yourself the opportunity. Your kids need you to be *in one piece,* and whatever you do to help hold yourself together is necessary to your being emotionally strong *for them.*

Megan married Jack when she was twenty. Three years later, when Vince was born, Jack suggested she quit her job and become a stay-at-home mom. But Megan, wanting to contribute to the family income and to keep her brain busy, opted for a compromise: a home-based business. She began assembling and selling customized gift baskets, a job she could work at from home while caring for Vince, and after the arrival of Shelley, their second child.

Two years later, Megan began to suspect that her husband had a gambling addiction. When confronted, Jack denied the addiction and denied diverting household funds, though by then, Megan had solid proof. Even worse, Jack became verbally abusive. For eighteen tense months, Megan pressed the issue to no avail. Money continued to disappear. Jack remained in denial and remained abusive. He refused to go for help — either marital counseling or counseling for the addiction he still denied. Things at home went from bad to worse, till finally Megan hired an attorney and filed divorce papers. Jack reluctantly moved out.

Megan's income from the gift basket business and the court-mandated support payments was not enough to provide for her and the kids. She kept the business going while she sought and found a nine-to-five job. But childcare costs badly ate into the income she derived, and Megan found it was still difficult making ends meet.

What's more, the kids' behavior showed the stress of having their father move out of the house and not having their mother around as much. Vince was in school all day, yet he seemed affected worse than Shelley. Megan, exhausted after a day's work and the tiring drive home in traffic, tried valiantly to spend all her evening time with the kids — at least until their bedtime — to help them cope with the radical changes in their lives.

After the kids went to bed, Megan would do as much advance prep work on the next night's dinner as was feasible, do laundry or housecleaning or whatever other chores were necessary, and put in time on her gift basket orders as well.

She took no time for herself, but she downplayed the need. The kids had to come first, she told herself. Besides, she had expected life to be easier once Jack moved out, so she thought she wouldn't need to pamper herself. No longer would money be missing. No longer would there be the stress of the constant hostility she had endured. Yet Megan found that her level of stress remained high.

She began snapping at the kids. When they whined that they wanted their daddy or became angry or cranky over a trivial matter, instead of sympathizing or soothing, Megan barked that she would not put up with whining or meted out punishments for unacceptable behavior. Things quickly went from bad to worse.

One night her best friend showed up at her door unexpectedly. "I'm watching the kids. You're going out," she announced in a tone that brooked no argument. "Go to a movie. Go visit another friend. Go wander at the mall. But *go.*"

"The kids need me," Megan protested.

"They need you to be yourself," her friend answered. "They need you to be in one piece. And you're not." After some brief further discussion, Megan reluctantly went out for an evening of R&R. She returned refreshed and better able to deal with her kids and with life in general. Was one evening out a miracle cure? Definitely not. But it was a start.

And by breaking the vicious cycle and seeing the results, Megan came to realize that she was doing her kids no good if she spent every minute with them to the detriment of her own emotional well-being. She needed some Megan-time, some down time, some time to herself in which she could unwind.

Though Jack's departure had solved a lot of problems for Megan, it had created new ones, from work exhaustion, to the need to be the sole on-premises parent to her two kids, to dealing with their misbehavior because Daddy was gone. The toxic atmosphere of his constant anger and nastiness had cleared, but in its wake there were other problems. Megan never regretted asking Jack to leave, but she was amazed and dragged down by the unexpected difficulties that ensued. She had unrealistically expected clear sailing once her husband was out of the house.

Once she stepped back and got a better view of what she was facing, how she was reacting, and the fact that she was not doing Vince and

Shelley any good by being there for them all the time, but in a bad place in her head, she re-ordered her priorities. Megan made sure that she had occasional nights out, even if it meant leaving the kids home with a sitter. She learned to take some time for herself, and not only was she better off for it, the kids were too.

Teach Them Resilience

One of the most valuable things you can do for your children as they grow up with the challenges of your divorce and single parenthood is to help them build resilience. The ability to bounce back — exactly what you're doing as you create your own life after the divorce — is an invaluable resource that will serve them throughout their lives. A few tips:

❖ *Give them a strong set of moral values.* We're not talking religion here — that is your call, of course. With or without a religious component, they can learn the importance of honesty, integrity, faithfulness, loyalty, and dedication to a worthy cause.

❖ *Teach them how to stay healthy* and take care of themselves. Exercise, nutrition, sleep, balance — all the things we're advocating for you — are the foundation of success in any endeavor they may undertake, from school to career to relationships.

❖ *Let them know that life will often present unexpected obstacles,* and that they have the personal strength to jump those hurdles. If you protect them from every adversity — always chauffeuring them to school and activities, bailing them out when they face difficult situations with friends or school or money, or excusing their "minor" infractions — how will they learn to take responsibility for themselves, and to face the "big ones" that will inevitably come up later in life?

❖ *Let them make mistakes.* The ones they make now will hurt but won't likely have life-long consequences. They'll learn from their errors, and they'll learn how to deal with minor failures. Better now than when mistakes can have major consequences in their adult life.

❖ *Don't always bail them out.* Be there for them when they get into trouble, but give them a chance to work it out. Let them pay for that broken window, maybe by mowing the owner's lawn for a few weeks.

❖ *Go to bat for them.* Does this sound contradictory? There are times when your intervention will be necessary. Schools do what they can to give kids good educational opportunities, but like other human institutions, they're not always perfect. There are times when a parent's assertiveness is necessary to help get the job done. You'll teach your kids a valuable lesson in dealing with authority and institutions if you stand up for them when the system fails them.

❖ *Let them know they always have your love.* That solid foundation will make all the difference in giving them the strength to keep on in the face of adversity. A strong support system is one of the most important factors in personal resilience.

Your divorce has probably been rough on your kids, but it's not the end of their world. They can grow up healthy, live happy productive lives, and prosper like anyone else. And you're going to see to it that they do!

AfterWords — Chapter Seven

Key Points in the Chapter

- Divorced moms often make the mistake of trying to "make it up" to their children by spoiling or smothering them.

- We all have only so many hours. Working moms need to allow time for themselves as well as for their children.

- If you don't take care of yourself, you won't be able to take care of your children.

- Resilience is one of the most important gifts you can "give" your children; help them learn how to "bounce back" from life's inevitable adversities.

Activity of the Week

- Ask a relative or friend to care for your children for two hours sometime this week. Take that time to relax, sit in the park and read a book, get a massage, have coffee with a lifeline friend, go fishing, catch up on thank-you notes, take a bike ride....

- Have a Family Council meeting to discuss ways to deal with adversity. Talk about real problems family members have confronted, or make up hypothetical situations if necessary. Help the kids to figure out simple steps they can take when difficult problem circumstances come up.

Suggested Readings and Resources

American Psychological Association (2004). *The Road to Resilience.* Washington, DC: APA. (Free brochure. Order at www. apahelpcenter.org)

Emery, R.E. (2004). *The Truth About Children and Divorce: Dealing with the Emotions So You and Your Children Can Survive.* New York: Viking/Penguin.

Heatherington, E. M. and Kelly, J (2002). *For Better or for Worse: Divorce Reconsidered.* New York: W.W. Norton.

Lansky, V. (1989). *Vicki Lansky's Divorce Book for Parents: Helping Your Children Cope With Divorce and Its Aftermath.* New York: Signet Books.

MacGregor, C. (2001). *The Divorce Helpbook for Kids.* Atascadero, CA: Impact Publishers.

MacGregor, C. (2004). *The Divorce Helpbook for Teens.* Atascadero, CA: Impact Publishers.

MacGregor, C. (2005). *Jigsaw Puzzle Family: The Stepkids' Guide to Fitting It Together.* Atascadero, CA: Impact Publishers.

Stahl, P. (2000). *Parenting After Divorce.* Atascadero, CA: Impact Publishers.

8

• • • • • • • • •

If Your Kids Are With You

EVEN WITH YOUR LOVE AND SUPPORT, your children are bound to bump up against some obstacles as they deal with the emotional and practical aspects of the divorce. This chapter will help you to help them.

You may be reading this early on in the process of the divorce, so we've started with some tips on telling them what's happening. Among the other issues discussed here: explaining what the divorce will mean to them; helping them deal with Dad no longer living with your family; responding to their emotional stress; coping with the shuffle between two houses; getting their help with chores; improving communication with family meetings.

This material pretty much assumes the children are living with you. (More than twenty-five percent of children are being raised by a single parent today.) In the next chapter, we'll talk about issues that come up if you are *not* the primary custodial parent.

Have You Told Them?

By the time you're reading this, you probably are either already divorced or in the process of divorcing, and your kids know about the split. Before you go on to the next section, however, you might skim this to be sure you've gotten the most important information across to them.

What is most important in explaining the divorce to the kids? Two main points stand above all else, and the kids need to hear them no matter how old they are:

❖ The divorce is in no way their fault.

❖ Both of you will always go on loving them.

"The Divorce Is Not Your Fault"

Perhaps you understand the necessity of communicating these points to a six-year-old or ten-year-old but not a teenager. Perhaps you think teenagers are old enough, and have enough friends from divorced homes, that they surely understand this divorce is in no way their fault.

Think harder. Here's a real-life scenario that will make the point vividly:

> Zac is a pretty typical fifteen-year-old: His room is a total shambles. He barely says two words to his parents, spends (in their opinion) entirely too much time at the computer and playing video games, and eats way too much junk food. (His mom never buys this stuff, but Zac uses his allowance to supply himself with high-fat, high-salt, empty-calorie snacks.)
>
> Naturally, he's caught a lot of flak over the last few years for all these behaviors, especially from his dad.
>
> In the last half year or so, as things grew more tense between Zac's parents while their marriage was falling apart, Zac's dad's temper flared readily. Dad lost patience with Zac frequently, and there were more confrontations between the two over the state of Zac's room, the noise of his stereo, his study habits, and all the other things that typically exasperate the parents of teens. Zac's father was overreacting to Zac's behaviors because of the tension in his marriage, but Zac didn't realize that. All he knew was that Dad was *never* happy with him anymore, and the household seemed the scene of an ongoing battle.
>
> Then Zac's parents announced that they were getting a divorce. Dad would be moving to an apartment nearby. Zac would continue to live with Mom.
>
> Zac's reaction? He honestly believed that Dad had become so fed up with him that Dad was moving out just to get away from Zac!
>
> Unfortunately, being a teenager and therefore not the most open communicator, Zac didn't express these feelings to either of his parents. And, also typical of teenagers, he thought it was all about him. He became depressed, which his parents ascribed to the divorce itself. Neither of them realized the heavy — and totally misplaced — burden of guilt that Zac had shouldered.
>
> Fortunately, a caring teacher referred Zac to the school guidance counselor. Zac eventually admitted to the counselor his belief that he had caused the divorce. The counselor invited Zac's parents to come in for a family conference. Both parents showed up for the meeting (even though

Zac's dad had by now moved out), and Zac was helped to understand that the divorce was in no way his fault.

"I thought you understood that, honey!" his mom said. "You know a divorce is between the husband and the wife."

"But Dad was so unhappy with me. Nothing I did was right for him," Zac explained. "He used to say, 'I can't take it anymore.' So I thought that was why he left."

Might your child arrive at a similar erroneous conclusion? Even if he or she is, like Zac, "old enough to know better"? Don't let that happen. Kids need to understand that the divorce is in no way the result of anything they've done. And they also need to know that they can't do anything to change the facts.

Kids sometimes try to bargain: "If I promise to eat all my vegetables will Daddy stay?" "If I promise to always do my chores will you two stay married?" Your kids need to understand that the divorce is neither their fault nor anything they have any control over.

"Mom and Dad Will Always Love You"

The other key point is equally important: Your kids need to be reassured that even though Dad and Mom don't love each other any more, neither you nor your ex will ever stop loving them.

Both parents have to sign off on this one. *Don't lie to your kids.*

This is vital information to get across, whether or not your kids express this concern to you out loud. Trust us, this worry is going to be running around inside their heads, even if they don't verbalize it. They need to know that Mom will always be Mom, Dad will always be Dad, and both of you will always love them. Unless....

He's Really Gone

But what if your husband left you and the kids, perhaps moved away, and made it clear that he's finished with you as a family?

Though this doesn't happen often, it does happen on occasion, sad to say. Again, the primary things for you to accomplish are to make sure that the kids understand that Daddy didn't leave because of anything they did, and to make sure that they see you as being there for them, a rock-solid presence in their lives, and one whose love is unending. If they can't count on their father remaining in their lives, they need more than ever to know you are a constant, unswerving part of their lives, now and forever.

Jeremy was eight when his parents broke up. Jeremy's dad, who married quite young, had been truly unready for the responsibilities of marriage, and when he finally ended the marriage, he decided he'd had enough of fatherhood, too. Immature and selfish, he told his now ex-wife, "The kid'll be better off without me." It was a cop-out, of course, an obligation dodge. What he meant was that he was no longer willing to shoulder the responsibility of being a father.

Jeremy's father moved in with his brother, not half an hour's drive from Jeremy and his mom, but he never came to visit. The courts saw to it that he paid his child support check — the money was taken out of his paycheck — but that was the only obligation he honored.

Jeremy's mom expected Jeremy to act out, to react to his father's disappearance with misbehavior. She was fully prepared for rebelliousness, sullenness, defiance . . . all the behaviors she'd observed from her nephew when his parents had divorced.

To her amazement, Jeremy began behaving *better* than ever. He did his homework without being told, kept his room fairly clean, offered to do chores around the house, fed and walked the dog, and offered to start doing the dishes, too.

His demeanor changed, too; he was quiet and more withdrawn than before. He wasn't his usual happy self (that part was understandable). Though pleased with his behavior, his mother was surprised by it. So surprised, in fact, that she decided to consult a professional. It just didn't seem normal for Jeremy to be this well-behaved. "Maybe I shouldn't look a gift horse in the mouth," she said, trying to make light of her concerns.

But the therapist was on the same wavelength. "Without talking to your son, I can do no more than speculate. But I would guess that he's afraid you'll leave him too. He's on his best behavior in an effort to make sure you stay around. Try reassuring him that you're not going to leave him . . . no matter what. And if that doesn't bring about a change in his behavior, we should seriously consider having him come in to see me."

Jeremy's mom did as the counselor had suggested, and within a few weeks she saw a return to Jeremy's former normal behavior. Once he had been truly reassured that Mom wasn't going to desert him, he began to act like his old self: sloppy about room-cleaning, putting off doing his homework, not keeping up with his chores, and all the other things kids normally do that drive their parents buggy.

"Couldn't leave well enough alone, could you?" his aunt remarked wryly when her sister brought her up to date on the change in Jeremy's behavior.

But Jeremy's mom was actually relieved to see Jeremy being a normal kid again. Though it meant more work for her and more clashes between them, she knew it was a sign that he was feeling more secure.

Not All Dads Are Deadbeats

Sometimes a father absents himself for practical or emotional reasons. A major promotion, job change, or transfer may result in his moving out of the area. A move may be born of economic necessity. On the emotional side, an ex-husband may be devastated at being divorced by his wife, find it too unbearable to remain living near her in his old community, and opt to move out of the area.

But the father who absents himself in this manner doesn't cut himself off from his kids. He may not be able to see them often, but he does see them when he can, even if it's only once or twice a year. And he keeps in touch between visits — by phone, e-mail, text messaging, postal mail, packages and photographs. If Dad can afford it, he may set up a webcam so that his kids can see him through the computer. Digital cameras and cell phones with cameras are another increasingly popular option for "being there." And who knows what tomorrow's technology will bring?

The kids in this type of situation will miss their father more than the kids whose dad lives around the corner or across town and sees them often. They may need some reassurance that dad still loves them, even though he can't visit them often. But they aren't in the same bad spot as the kids whose father simply turned his back and walked away.

Of course, sometimes the father lives far away because Mom moved away and took the kids with her. Again, this may be for economic, emotional or practical reasons. It may be that she needed to move in with her mother, her sister, or a friend, in order to have help with childcare so she could go back to work. Maybe she simply needed to move somewhere where living is cheaper. Or maybe she couldn't take staying in the town where the now-split family was well known.

If that's you we've just described, the kids may resent you for moving them away from their dad. They may even resent him for not moving when you did, so he could still live near them. Your challenge is to help them stay in close touch with their father, even though he may not be on your list of "Top Ten Favorite People." Or perhaps you had a marvelously amicable divorce and remained friends. Either way, he's still the kids' dad, and you need to keep in mind that if you fail to help them keep in touch with their dad, you're hurting them, your ex, and yourself. Yes, yourself, because eventually they may resent you for undermining their relationship with their dad, or at least not helping to promote it.

Whatever your gripes are with your ex, remember that he is still the kids' father, and the kids need a father. Even if he is not the best father on this planet, unless he is outright abusive, he is better than no dad, and the kids will be the better for having a relationship with him. (At some point they will come to appreciate *you* for facilitating their relationship with their dad. By helping them, you're helping your own standing in your kids' eyes.) Remember, this isn't about your ex, your feelings toward him, or what kind of person you think he is. This is about the kids and their need for a dad. And even if you eventually remarry, and choose someone who is a marvelous father figure to the kids, they will still be better off knowing you have not cut off access to their biological dad.

"Why Doesn't Daddy Ever Come to See Us Any More?"

Let's take a look at the father who neglects his kids. We are not talking here about the father who moves away and totally shuns the kids. (More about that rascal in a moment.) The father under discussion now is the dad who lives reasonably nearby, yet often finds reasons that he cannot see the kids when he is scheduled to. He may be working overtime or just vaguely "too busy," or he may say that he has no money to do anything with them or offer some other reason for not seeing them. It isn't that he *never* sees them, but he misses more visiting days than he shows up for. He rarely phones to talk to the kids. Perhaps he forgets their birthdays, and he fails to acknowledge other milestones or congratulate them on accomplishments (earning awards in school and merit badges in Scouts, getting chosen for the marching band, scoring a goal, or getting all A's on a report card). He shows up often enough to keep their hopes up, and seldom enough that they are often disappointed and hurt.

What can you do?

First, you need to make sure that the kids understand that it is not because of any flaw in them that their father is ignoring them. It is not that they are unlovable, that they have done anything wrong, that they have let him down in any way; *it is not their fault.* Try to say something neutral, such as, "It's too bad Dad didn't get to see you this weekend. I bet he misses you," which carries the message that Dad *would* like to see them. If they are too old (and wise) to believe that, then tell them straight out, "The important thing I want you to realize is that, whatever Dad's reason for not seeing you, it's nothing *you've* done. You're great kids. And it's *his* loss if he doesn't see you. I know it's your loss, too, but Dad's cheating himself by not spending time with his wonderful kids." Reinforce the message by being loving and caring and demonstrative. Having a mother who loves them and shows it will go a long way toward helping their self-image.

This does *not* mean lavishing them with gifts or letting them "get away with murder" in terms of discipline. That is *not* the way to show a child your love. Enforce the rules you've set up. Give only a reasonable number of gifts. Don't give in to every plea of "Buy me this," or "I want that." But be there for them, show them you love them, and be a steady and consistent force in their lives.

Second, do what you can to fill the father void in their lives. There are certain activities that traditionally have fallen to dads but could be assumed by you or another woman — such things as teaching your kids how to pitch and bat, or taking them fishing if that interests them. What's important is that they have *someone* to do these things for them. Whether that someone is a father figure, a man whose place in their lives is otherwise casual at best, or a woman is irrelevant.

Some Dads Are Best Left to History

What of the father who deserves to be cut off from access? What if your ex is an abuser? What if he beat the kids, or worse? In that case, you probably have some sort of court judgment that keeps him from seeing the kids, whether the judge in the divorce proceedings terminated your ex's parental rights, or there is a restraining order against him that keeps him away from the kids (and presumably from you too).

In that case *you* are not the person responsible for cutting off the kids' access. Make sure they understand that this was done by a higher authority than you, someone you have to answer to just as the kids have to answer to you. And let them know that the court did so for a reason: Dad was not a good person. Don't be surprised if the kids still want to see their father, abusive though he may be. This sometimes happens. Explain to them that the judge wants to help keep the kids safe, and Daddy's behavior makes it not safe for them to be around him.

What About a Proxy Father?

Another thing you can do for your kids when a father is totally absent from their lives is to provide a "proxy" father, a male figure they can look up to, emulate, and talk to. Someone who can be a father-figure in their lives, or at very least a positive male role model. This might be your brother, your father, a neighbor, a co-worker, a coach, a youth leader, a "Big Brother," the husband of a friend of yours, or a male friend of yours. ("Male friend," incidentally, need not be a romantic partner. Cynthia MacGregor has a number of platonic male friends — several of them close friends — whose friendship she treasures.)

Even if their dad is active and involved in their lives, he probably doesn't visit with them as often as they'd like. They need and want to be out on the lawn, at the park, or on the street of your cul-de-sac, pitching, batting, fielding fly balls and grounders, shooting hoops, dribbling, kicking a soccer ball, riding a bike, and skateboarding. So even if their dad is an active and involved father, offering someone additional as a coach, mentor, or fishing buddy is a good idea. And of course, that person could easily be you, if you're good at these things.

Whether it's this same person or a different one, try also to have an appropriate person show up for the kids at such occasions as the church's father-daughter dance, the soccer league's dad-and-son banquet, and at any other time that a father's physical presence is called for.

Don't be surprised, though, if your kids choose their own father figure. Your children may form a special bond with the father of a friend, a neighbor, a youth group leader, a teacher or other school staff member, or perhaps even a local merchant. And that's fine, as long as they choose wisely, and as long as the person they've chosen is agreeable to assuming the role, and you are comfortable with this person. (Have a talk with him to be sure he's okay with the relationship! It can be demanding of time and emotional energy.)

"But WHY Are We Getting a Divorce, Mommy?"

What if the kids ask *why* you're getting divorced? This is a logical question, and one they will very likely ask, out of natural curiosity. Of course, it's one you don't really want to answer in any great detail. Even if your husband was cheating on you and you're very hurt and angry, telling the kids of his misdeeds will not help them. You may think it would serve him right if the kids turned against him, but *it would not be in the kids' best interest.* And this is about what's best for the kids, not about what would give you wicked satisfaction.

If you and your husband argued frequently in front of the kids, you can tell them that you and Dad didn't get along very well. The kids understand that nobody is happy when there's a lot of arguing going on. They can sense that it isn't good for anyone — including the kids themselves. You can make it clear to them that it's better if you and Dad don't live together anymore.

If your arguing was done in private, or if that type of discord was not the reason behind the breakup, you can simply tell the kids that it's a private matter between you and their dad. Reassure the kids that it *is* between you two and has nothing to do with them or anything they did.

You also will want to talk to them about any changes that you know lie ahead that will affect them. If you are moving as a result of the divorce, or going back to work, or shifting from part-time work to full-time, or if there is any other significant change in the patterns of their lives as a result of the divorce, be sure to tell them, and give them a chance to express their concerns.

Don't trivialize the changes. Without making it all sound ominous and scary, you can acknowledge the seriousness of these changes and honor the kids' concerns. "Who will take care of us when we get home from school if you'll be at work?" "How can I visit with my friends if we have to move away?" "If we're going to live with Grandma, what about Petey? You know Grandma doesn't like dogs."

Answer the kids' questions honestly, and be as reassuring as you can be within the scope of honesty, but don't make light of their concerns.

"But Daddy Lets Us Stay Up Late!"

Another common change after a divorce is a tightening of the budget. If there are going to be fewer trips to the local pizzeria or the movies, or you have to give up your summer cabin, or the kids are going to have to make do with fewer clothes and less expensive ones, let them know this too. *But,* don't take the tack of, "It's not my fault. Blame Daddy." Even if he *was* the one who wanted out of the marriage, against your wishes, and you now resent him for the predicament you find yourself in, *don't try to turn the kids against him*. Nobody wins in the blame game.

Don't be surprised, either, if your ex suddenly begins lavishing presents and expensive expeditions on the kids, trying to buy their love. The father who moves out — especially when it's by his own choice, but often even when it's not — may be bothered by guilt, or simply by a fear that the kids won't love him as much when he's not around all the time. In addition, many divorced dads see themselves as being in competition with Mom. Though they may not ask the kids this question outright, they're thinking, "Who do you love more, Mom or me?"

These dads try to buy the kids' affections, attention, and partisanship, or simply try to overcome their own guilt, by giving the kids whatever they want — clothing, toys, videogames, junk food — or taking them to theme parks, ball games, shows, or other attractions the kids enjoy. Such fathers are known by various monikers: "Uncle Daddy, the Ice-Cream Man" behaves like a rich, spoiling uncle, not a disciplinary parent, and always buys the kids ice cream and other treats. "Disneyland Dad" spends custody weekends taking his kids off to the nearest amusement park, regardless of the cost. (The female equivalent is "Mall Mom," or "Mama Softouch," who spoils her kids through shopping trips.)

Fortunately for you, the "Disneyland/Ice Cream" ploy works only for a while; after that, the kids catch on to the fact that the degree to which they're spoiled is not a measure of how much they are loved. And while it's great (for them!) that Daddy lets them stay up for an hour past their bedtime when they're at his house, they soon recognize that doesn't mean he loves them more than Mom does.

"I Hate This Divorce!"

Even if their dad is marvelous about seeing the kids at every scheduled visiting day, calls them on the phone nightly, sends them e-mail, and does everything right, he's not living there anymore. And even if you've provided the most marvelous proxy father figure for the kids — one who truly cares about them, sets a good example for them, does things with them, talks to them, and is just there for them in every way — they know he's not really their father. You can expect some emotional reaction from the kids...in any number of ways.

It might be that your child will express herself forthrightly, asking, "Why can't Daddy still live with us?" even though you've explained the divorce thoroughly and adequately. She might cry, or she might grow angry, or she may simply be sullen. She may blame you, your ex, or both of you, or she may vent her anger toward the family court judge or even God.

The child may not, on the other hand, realize what's upsetting her. She might be mean to her sister, kick the cat, be uncooperative around the house, or in some other way act out. Her anger may be inappropriate, or disproportionate to the cause (such as if her sister did something that provoked her, but she reacted out of proportion to the mild offense). Or she may seem sad much of the time or simply uncooperative. If this is the sort of behavior you're seeing, it's a pretty safe guess that this is really about her father's absence from the household.

Your task is to be simultaneously firm and sympathetic. Firm in letting her know that aggressive or other inappropriate behaviors will not be tolerated, even when she's in emotional pain.

Sympathetic in letting her know that yes, you do understand that she misses Dad, that she's hurting, and that she's totally justified in her feelings. But lashing out aggressively or dumping on other people is not an appropriate or acceptable reaction.

Remember, too, that each kid will react differently, depending on personality, age, gender, and even such matters as how many of his or her friends come from divorced homes. A teenager has a better ability to comprehend that this isn't about her...yet, because she's going through a period of turmoil and high emotional sensitivity, she may react more strongly. A younger child will have less comprehension of the realities of divorce...yet, because the hormones and emotions of the teen years haven't yet kicked in, he may be calmer. One child may blame his father, another blame her mother, regardless of who initiated the divorce. One child may react primarily with anger, another primarily with weepy sadness, another primarily with withdrawal.

Help Them Deal with It

Find ways to help your kids deal with their feelings.

First of all, try to get them to talk about what they're feeling. It's best, of course, if they can talk to you. But if they perceive you as the villain (*"You* made Daddy leave!"), if they're afraid of adding to your burden, or if for any other reason they aren't comfortable opening up to you, find someone else they can talk to: a caring relative or friend of the family, the youth group director or clergyperson, a sympathetic school guidance counselor, or any other supportive and sensible person they can relate to. And if they seem more troubled than they should be by the divorce, consider getting professional help for them — a few sessions with a counselor or therapist.

There are other ways you can help them:

❖ Provide a diary or journal in which they can record their innermost feelings.

❖ Encourage them to write more creatively — perhaps a poem about divorce or about sadness or anger, a short story, or an essay. Anything to help them express their feelings can be helpful.

❖ If they're too young to write, or if they don't express themselves well verbally, encourage them to draw. You can suggest they draw a "picture of a divorced family" or just a picture of anything they want. Their feelings will be expressed through their art, whether it's a dark, gloomy scene that mirrors their current state of mind or a sunny depiction that reflects their hope for better days ahead.

❖ Rent a three-hanky movie they can watch and cry over — with or without you, whichever you think will leave them more comfortable about crying. Getting the tears out is good. A movie about an animal that gets lost or that dies allows them to cry for a lost dog or horse while shedding real tears for their "lost" father or their "lost" close-knit family.

❖ If they have puppets, suggest they put on a puppet show. You can suggest it be about a family going through divorce, or about "something that's important," or you can leave the topic to their discretion. If they don't have puppets, you can buy them some inexpensive ones or even make sock puppets, paper finger-puppets, or potato puppets, or use stuffed animals.

❖ Even without puppets, the kids can put on a play. If you have only one child, this is a less useful choice. In order to have at least one other cast member, your "only" will need to involve a friend, and that friend is likely to want to have the play be about some topic other than divorce, family issues, absent fathers, or other related topics. (Unless, of course, the other child's family is going through something similar.)

❖ Do you know a child whose parents were divorced long enough ago that the child is now in a happier, more accepting frame of mind, more used to the new circumstances of his or her family? This might be a friend or classmate of one of your kids, the son or daughter of divorced friends or neighbors, a cousin or other family member, someone your kids and/or you know from church, temple, school or scouts, or possibly even the kids' babysitter. Ask this person if he or she would be willing to talk candidly with your kids about the ups and downs of being the child of divorced parents, about coping strategies, and simply about the fact that the raw edges do smooth out after a while. When *you* say, "It won't seem so bad in a month or two," the kids may think, "Yeah, sure — what does she know?!" But, when another kid — one who's "been there, done that, and brought home the T-shirt" — says it, the kids will give it more credence. (Incidentally, such conversations probably need to be more than a one-time event; if a helping relationship develops, it will likely involve a series of such talks.)

❖ Talk to your divorced friends or acquaintances who have kids and find out what worked best for them in helping their kids learn to cope and to adjust to the new situation. You'll probably get lots of ideas for handling specific problems and situations that aren't addressed in this book.

❖ Seriously consider whether professional therapy might be appropriate, particularly with a child and family therapist who is highly experienced with divorce. You should know that family therapists almost always want to include the whole family in the process, so it won't be a matter of "sending" your child to therapy once a week. Plan to take part yourself. (For help in finding a qualified therapist, see Appendix II.)

One final thought about helping your kids to deal with their emotions in times of stress. Whether it's a movie, play, poem, or heart-to-heart talk, don't assume that a single event — even if accompanied by a waterfall of tears — will resolve your child's grief over loss of her or his father. Sincere expression of those sad feelings is normal: "Of course you miss your dad. I know you feel really sad that he's gone. Everybody feels unhappy when someone they love goes away." It's important to provide continuing opportunities for the kids to express their sadness, anger, and feelings of loss. Don't brush off, ignore, or hush their sighs, withdrawal, tears, or outbursts. Be as accepting as you can, and let them know you're there for them when they need your emotional support — for as long as it takes.

He's Still Their Dad

If your husband was cruel (or merely unkind), neglectful, unfaithful, or some other negative trait — that is, if your divorce resulted from some specific misbehavior on his part, and not just from an incompatibility, or from one of you "falling out of love" with the other — you may be actively happy to have him out of the house. But remember that this reflects *your* experience with him and *your* relationship to him. The *kids'* relationship to him, though, was something quite different. And even if he was neglectful of them too, or sometimes unkind, they still love him. He's their dad, after all, no matter what his faults are. So please don't lose sight of the fact that, no matter how relieved or happy you may be to be on your own again, the kids' feelings don't mirror yours. And, in fact, you should temper your expression of such feelings around the kids. Save your abundant joy over the new and happier situation for when you're with your friends. Around the kids, you don't have to pretend to be sorry your ex is gone, but don't be gleeful either. They will not react positively to "Mom's glad that Daddy's gone."

Don't Make Them the "Puny" Express

In fact, if you are happy that he's gone — and sometimes even if you aren't — you may prefer to have as little to do with him as possible. Whether because you're glad to be shed of him, because you're angry that he left you, or simply because talking to him is so damned uncomfortable and awkward, you may be tempted to avoid necessary conversations with him and, instead, send messages through the kids.

In a word: *Don't.*

It's totally unfair to make the kids into messengers. It's also likely that they'll get your message, or his reply, garbled when they deliver it. But that's not the main reason for not turning them into little couriers. *Speak for yourself.* Asking them to carry messages is really imposing an unfair burden. This is especially true if the message is an unpleasant one, or one that might lead to controversy: "Where is the child support check?" "Don't send Alicia home with mismatched socks again." "We're going away next weekend. You'll have to see the kids some other time." But even neutral messages — "I have somewhere to go next Sunday. My friend Tanya will bring the kids to you at the usual time" — should be delivered by you, not by the kids.

Even worse than turning them into message carriers is turning the kids into spies. Of course, you may well be curious about what's going on in your ex-husband's life, especially if you have a specific question. If he was the one who initiated the divorce, you may be wondering now if he ever has second thoughts and misses you.

Many mothers in that position will pump their kids for information: "Does Daddy seem happy?" "Does Daddy talk about me at all? What does he say?"

Then there are the women who feel their ex-husbands aren't shouldering a fair share of the financial burden. It may be that the ex is paying exactly what the court mandated but not a penny more, even under extraordinary circumstances of need. It may be that the woman suspects her ex now has a better-paying job or second job, perhaps "under the table" to avoid having his support payments raised. And in that situation, a woman may ask her kids, "Does Daddy have any new furniture?" "Is Dad wearing a whole lot of new clothes?" "Does Daddy still drive the same old car?"

Then there is the woman who wonders if her ex has met someone new. She may ask her kids, "What other grownups were over at Daddy's house while you were there?" "Does Dad have any new friends you've met? Are they women?" Or even, "Did you notice any women's clothes or shoes in Daddy's closet?" "Did you see any stuff like lipstick or makeup around the house?"

Though it's tempting to peek into your ex's home and his life via the eyes of your kids, don't do it. The kids' reactions may vary. Some kids realize they're being asked to "tattle" on their dads, and they resent it. Other kids feel puffed up with importance at being able to provide Mom with information that's obviously valuable to her. Many kids feel both these emotions simultaneously.

But it isn't fair to the kids, nor do you want them to think asking or answering such questions is all right. (After all, your ex may be asking them questions about *you*, too!)

Not that *all* questions are bad. "Is Daddy well?" is a valid question. It shows the kids that you still care that their father is healthy. "What did you do this weekend with Daddy?" is a fair question, too. It's reasonable for you to want to know how your kids spent their weekend. Besides, it's a normal motherly thing to try to make conversation with your kids about what's going on in their lives. "What did you have for dinner?" is a reasonable question; you want to know that the kids are eating right even when they're away from home.

But that's where it stops. Snoopy, spying, prying questions that ask the kids to "rat" on their dad, or that will impel them to go on a spy expedition through his house the next time they visit, are wrong for a variety of reasons. This is not a fair position to put them in. Neither is it fair for them to be put in the middle if you two still have unresolved issues.

The New Woman in His Life

Sooner or later, it's bound to come up. Is there a new woman in your ex's life? At some point, he's likely to meet someone with whom he'll get involved in a serious relationship. They could start living together; maybe even marry. How are the kids going to handle it? He's almost certainly going to be dating women, and at some point the kids will become aware of that, too. How are they going to handle that? How will you?

Very often, kids will resent the new woman in Dad's life. They'll feel Daddy is being disloyal to you. Even if you secretly harbor some of the same feelings, you need to impress on the kids that this isn't so. Although they very probably hold hopes that you'll get back together, they need to know that isn't going to happen. Now that you and Dad are divorced, you're both free people. He's certainly free to date other women if he wants to, and you're free to see other men. (If you try to foster feelings of misplaced loyalty in the kids, in terms of resenting Dad for dating, this indoctrination is likely to turn around and bite you when you start dating and the kids feel *you're* being unfair to *Dad*.)

And if he marries again? That's a broad enough topic for a whole other book. For now, suffice it to say that, even if the news hits you with the force of a hundred-pound sack of concrete, you need to encourage the kids to be happy for Dad. (What? You never took acting lessons as a child? Well give it your best shot anyway!)

Chores and Allowances

On a much more mundane level, let's talk about such everyday matters as chores around the house. When you and your husband split up, your children, unless they're extremely young, are likely to find more household chores apportioned to them. Did your ex used to do some household tasks that one or all of your kids are old enough to take over? Have you taken over his chores, but it's too much of a load for you on top of what you already were doing?

Have you gone back to work, or shifted from part-time work to full-time? You could use a little relief from some of those burdens!

Depending on their ages and abilities, the kids can take over one, several, or many of the chores that formerly were yours and/or your husband's. From taking out the garbage to walking the dog, from washing the car to washing the dishes, from setting the table to clearing the table to doing some of the cooking or at least the food prep (peeling potatoes, washing lettuce, trimming the fat from the chicken), there are chores that are age-appropriate for your kids. Are they old enough to do the laundry? Can they make their own beds in the morning? Dust their own rooms...or the whole house? Run the vacuum? Shovel snow in winter and rake leaves in autumn? Empty the dishwasher? If they're teenagers, perhaps they can do some grocery-shopping for you, cook some dinners, do some of the ironing and mending, and mop the floors. Hey, these are all things that must be done to keep the family going. Why shouldn't your capable youngsters share that load?

Of course, with all that extra responsibility, it's only fair to bump up their allowance if that's feasible, or to pay them directly for certain taxing chores. If you *can* afford to give them a raise in allowance commensurate with their increased tasks, we encourage you to do so. Allowance isn't just an entitlement. Some of the money you provide to your kids needs to be earned. And it isn't too early to teach your kids that hard work usually pays off financially. We live in an economy that expects everyone to work for their living. If kids learn that lesson — and companion lessons about saving and spending wisely — they'll have a huge jump on taking care of themselves as they become adults.

On the other hand, your divorce may leave you in such tight financial circumstances that the kids actually need to take a cut in their allowance. Or you may be able to avoid a cutback but be unable to give them a raise.

If that's the case, look for other, non-monetary ways to reward them. Perhaps an increase in privileges? "If you're going to undertake an increased share of the family task burden, it's only right that your privileges increase as well." Just what those privileges are is something you can best determine yourself. You might allow a child to eat snacks in his room, have friends over more often, stay up later, watch a more "adult" TV show, ride farther from home on her bike....

If you can't afford to increase their allowance, or even have to cut back, how are they going to get the spending money that every kid wants? Well, think back. How did you earn extra cash when you were young? There are some tried-and-true methods. Not every one will apply to every child — age and ability are certainly factors — but this list should prime the pump for ideas (exercise appropriate caution in helping them to screen prospective employers or customers):

❖ Wash dogs for neighbors and friends

❖ Wash cars for neighbors and friends

❖ Shovel snow (easy for us to say, here in South Florida and Central California!)

❖ Baby-sit or pet-sit or plant-sit for relatives and neighbors and friends

❖ Do yardwork — raking, weeding, trimming bushes, lawn mowing, vegetable-picking, pruning, or other gardening tasks

❖ Paint a fence or a shed for a neighbor, relative, or friend.

❖ Have a sidewalk sale — anything from the traditional lemonade stand to a sale of comic books and other books, old unwanted toys or games, or baked goods

❖ Collect recyclable materials, such as cans that litter the road, and turn them in to a for-profit recycling center that pays for such materials

❖ Deliver newspapers or advertising flyers

❖ Clean up the family business on weekends

❖ Help friends or neighbors or local small businesses with web sites. (Kids often know more about computers and the Internet than many adults.)

Starting with this list, your kids can probably come up with another dozen ideas of their own to begin their journey into the business world!

Family Council

What if the kids have a gripe, a question, or a quibble regarding this new distribution of chores, or the new amount of their allowance? What if they think they're entitled to more of a raise, or that the chores have been distributed unevenly, or that the allowance rollback is so totally unfair that you must be the meanest mom in creation?

Bring it up at a Family Council Meeting.

What's a Family Council Meeting? A businesslike meeting that might be held every Sunday after dinner, or once a month before Saturday chores, or simply whenever there's a need. Attendance is expected, though not forced, and absentees automatically forfeit any say in decisions made at the meeting. Keep the meeting short, be sure it stays under control like any good business meeting, but do let the kids speak their minds. (This doesn't mean they're entitled to endless complaints or arguments, but they can at least state their cases succinctly, once. There should be room for a little discussion, too.) If your kids are old enough, you can rotate the leadership so everyone has a chance to be in charge. Just like a real democracy!

A Family Council Meeting is the appropriate venue for announcements of various sorts: "Aunt Elayne and Uncle Lewis are coming to visit for a week next month." "The family is going to Colorado over spring break." "The stray dog we took in is pregnant — start looking for homes for puppies." "We're getting a new car."

A Family Council Meeting is the appropriate venue for subjects you want the kids' input on: "Our money is very limited these days. Do you want to go to camp for two weeks this summer, or go to the shore all together? We can't do both." "We're going away over winter break for a week. We can go to Grandma and Grandpa's, or we can go visit your cousins in Duluth. Those are your choices. Which do you prefer?" "Do we want to get a hamster or a guinea pig?" "We have to save some money. Would you rather give up cable TV or your cell phone?"

And a Family Council Meeting is the appropriate venue for kids to bring up complaints, requests, and comments: "I have too many chores. I can't do all that *and* get my homework done *and* get to bed on time…and I have *no time* to play or watch TV!" "I have more chores than Beth does. It's not fair!" "I'm entitled to more of an allowance for all the work I do around the house. My friend Ben gets a dollar more a week than I do, and he doesn't have to do anything but clean out the cat box and clear the table." "I don't have to do nearly as many chores at Daddy's house!"

Psychologists Dr. Gary McKay and Dr. Steven Maybell suggest the power of family meetings this way, in their popular book *Calming the Family Storm:*

> …*when family members know they have a definite time and place to bring up their concerns, to resolve issues, and to make plans, that assurance alone has the effect of reducing anger and conflict*…(p. 131)

We invite you to consider seriously starting regular family meetings at your house. You may be surprised at the results!

The Two-House Shuffle

Whether your kids live in a split-custody arrangement, spending roughly half their time at your house and half with your ex, or whether they live with you but visit your ex for weekends, holidays, and special occasions, there are bound to be different rules for the two houses. The potential for confusion and conflict is considerable. Don't depend on chance to work this out!

Maybe you make the kids eat a bite of everything you cook, but your ex lets them eat only what they want. Or maybe you cook only the foods you know they'll eat, but he serves them things they don't care for and insists they eat them anyhow. Maybe bedtime at your house is different than at Dad's. Perhaps you make them do more chores…or perhaps they have more chores at Dad's house than at yours, but one of the chores at your house is one they particularly despise — cleaning toilets comes to mind — whereas Dad has a housekeeper once a week. Perhaps they have to get up Sunday mornings to go to church at your house but are allowed to sleep late on Sundays at their father's. You get the idea. The rules are very likely to be different from one house to the other.

"But Daddy doesn't make us do that." "But Daddy lets us do this." "Daddy loves us more."

No, Daddy doesn't love them more. And the kids know it. It's an age-old ploy. Don't fall for it.

What to do?

Hold firm. Explain to them that Daddy is their parent and so are you. He has the right to make the rules he thinks are good for them at his house. And so do you at your home. You aren't going to always agree — that's one of the reasons you got divorced! You can't make Daddy do things your way, nor can Daddy make you do things his way. If they thought about it, they'd realize that you're stricter about some things, and Dad is probably stricter about others.

Of course, you *can't* make your ex do things your way, nor should you try (unless it's a matter of health or safety). If he habitually fills the kids with junk foods, or lets them do things you consider unsafe, you have a real reason to talk to him about it. (Trust your good judgment here. Young children shouldn't be riding their bikes unsupervised on a busy street, going out in cold or wet weather dressed inappropriately, or staying out late on school nights.) Otherwise, keep your thoughts to yourself, or confine your grousing to talks with your best friend, your sister, or your mother. You can't rule his life, and you can't tell him what rules to set for the kids. But remember, *he* can't tell *you* what to do either.

If there are genuine differences in your approach to raising your children, you'd best work those out in a formal parenting plan, such as is described at the end of chapter 12. Usually such a plan is worked out under supervision of the court, during the divorce negotiations. If you do not have such a plan, however, it's not too late to try to put one together with your ex. It could save you a lot of grief over the years to come.

The kids can and will understand that the rules are different in the two houses, and that "Daddy lets me" is not a valid reason for you to change your rules. If they "seem" not to grasp that, they may only be playing both ends against the middle. You can hardly blame them for seeing what they can get away with. Don't fall for it; hold firm.

Divorce Times Two

You might think that, having been through a divorce once before, it would be easier for the kids to handle it the second time around.

Don't bet on it.

Their father was wrenched out of their day-to-day life (no matter how active and involved he may still be with them). They probably bore a certain amount of resentment against him for leaving (whatever the circumstances of the divorce), and they may well have borne some resentment against you too (particularly if he left at your request and they know it).

Then you met someone else and married him. The kids may have latched on to your second husband quickly, though they were probably wary: *Is this one gonna stick around...or will he move out like Daddy did?* But eventually they accepted him. Eventually they may have grown to love him.

And now the two of you are breaking up.

It's not easy on you. But it's probably even tougher on the kids. And if you eventually marry for a third time, don't expect them to become easily attached to Husband Number Three.

Of course, if the kids were six months old and two years old when you and their father broke up, the impact on them from that divorce would have been much less. Or if they're now fifteen and seventeen when you're divorcing your second husband, by the time you incant, "The third time's the charm," as you march doggedly down the aisle, one or both are likely to be out of the house already.

But even without another remarriage, the second divorce itself is going to be rough on the kids. They're going to feel they've been let down twice, robbed of a father (or father figure) twice, deserted twice.

Starr and Rob were divorced when the children were four, six, and seven. The kids' reaction to the divorce was — for want of a better word — "typical," though there is no one standard reaction. Starr weathered the storm, and after the first half year — which was the worst — the kids began to acclimate to the new situation.

Still, raising three kids on her own was a tough go for Starr. Rob saw the kids on the prescribed visiting days, but most of the discipline, the homework help, and the day-to-day parenting fell on her shoulders. When she met Will, and it became obvious that he had serious relationship potential, Starr began thinking that it would be great to have a husband again…and some help in raising her daughter and two sons.

The kids were wary of Will at first, and upset when Starr announced she was planning to marry him. Even after he'd moved into the house, the kids were slow to accept him. The older boy at first protested, "I don't have to do what you say. You're not my *real* dad." And the girl asked if she could go live with her father. Starr said no, and Rob backed her up.

Eventually, though, the kids came around. The girl formed the strongest attachment to Will. She was a natural athlete, and the many hours Will spent helping her practice basketball and soccer won her over. He earned the boys' trust and respect more slowly, but he was a good stepdad, and eventually they were totally accepting of him and grew to love him.

Maybe Starr had jumped too quickly. Maybe she had married Will for the wrong reasons. At least, that was her take on the situation when, barely more than two years later, it became obvious that this was *not* the proverbial "match made in heaven." Citing "irreconcilable differences," Starr and Will agreed they'd be better off apart.

"At least this time won't be so tough on the kids," Starr said thankfully to her best friend. "It's not like it's their father moving out, this time."

Much to Starr's amazement, though, her daughter and older son seemed to take this divorce harder than the first one. Only the younger boy seemed indifferent. As that indifference showed itself in other aspects of his life, from school to his friends to his favorite TV shows, Starr surmised that, in his own way, he too was displaying a reaction to the divorce.

But at least he wasn't being obstinate, angry, sullen, and defiant, as the older two were. Starr finally sought family counseling for the three kids and herself; only after several months was some semblance of calm restored to the household.

"They feel they've been deserted twice. And they're blaming you," the counselor explained. "Your daughter feels she must be very unlovable, or both her dads wouldn't have moved out."

So if your kids react badly to your second divorce — perhaps even more strongly than they did to the first one, even though your second husband wasn't their biological father — don't be surprised.

Picking Up the Pieces

No doubt about it. Kids are strongly impacted by their parents' divorce, and they may not bounce back quickly. It's tough enough dealing with your own emotional and practical issues related to the divorce. Adding the stress of helping your kids through the process doubles the burden.

There is hope, however. If you take the time to listen carefully and understand where they're coming from, you can create conditions much more favorable to their recovery and growth in the wake of the divorce. Knowing that they'll be testing the limits, for example, you can steel yourself to hold firmly to the standards that are important to you. Knowing they will try to play Mom against Dad (even more than they did before the divorce!), you and your ex can agree to cooperate in supporting each other's house rules — even if they're different house rules. Knowing they need extra love and reassurance (such as, that you won't be leaving them also), you can look for special ways to let them know how important they are to you and how much you love them.

Remember that they're each unique individuals, and you have to treat them differently. Kenny at three does not understand as much as Karen at nine. That's not to say you don't have consistent standards — you should. But adapt your explanations to their age, gender, and ability to comprehend. And keep in mind that even teens don't yet have fully developed adult-level reasoning ability. Don't assume they have it figured out, even if they tell you they do!

More important than what they're *thinking* these days is how they're *feeling*. We're not suggesting it isn't necessary to explain to them what's happening. But it's even more critical that they feel loved by you, accepted by you, and reassured by you that you'll continue to be there for them.

Your children are precious, and they won't be young very long. Take advantage of every chance you have to nurture your loving relationship with them.

AfterWords — Chapter Eight

Key Points in the Chapter

- Your children know about the divorce, of course, but have you had a good heart-to-heart talk to reassure them that it's not their fault, and Mom and Dad will always love them?

- Watch carefully for signs that the kids may be having trouble adjusting: sleep problems, acting up, behaving "too well," self-blame, withdrawal. Some emotional reactions are normal, but they may need support to cope with extra stress at school, or with friends in the neighborhood, or just on their own.

- It's important to maintain a neutral-to-positive attitude toward your ex, for the sake of the children. Help them to see their father in as positive a light as you can.

- A "proxy father" may be a valuable addition to your kids' lives if their own dad is not available to them. Good male and female role models are important to both boys and girls.

- Don't lie to your kids, or make light of the seriousness of the changes in your family. They know things are not the same, and they're depending on you to help them understand what it means.

- Don't compete with your ex for your children's love. Everyone loses if you do.

- Don't ask them to carry messages back and forth. Communicate with each other as adults.

- If finances are tight, help the kids to learn about the value of work for pay. (But be cautious.)

- Hold occasional "family council" meetings with the kids to discuss issues and make decisions.

Activity of the Week

- Hold at least one family council meeting this week. Let one of the children lead the meeting, if he or she is old enough. Take notes and post them on the refrigerator. Follow up on any decisions the family makes.

Suggested Readings and Resources

Emery, R.E. (2004). *The Truth About Children and Divorce: Dealing with the Emotions So You and Your Children Can Survive.* New York: Viking/Penguin.

Lansky, V. (1989). *Vicki Lansky's Divorce Book for Parents: Helping Your Children Cope With Divorce And Its Aftermath.* New York: Signet Books.

McKay, G. and Maybell, S. (2004). *Calming the Family Storm: Anger Management for Moms, Dads, and All the Kids.* Atascadero, CA: Impact Publishers.

9

• • • • • • • • •

If Your Kids Are With Him... or Whom?

MOST OF THIS BOOK SO FAR has assumed that you have either minor children living with you or no kids at all. But of course, there are other possibilities. Your kids could live with your ex, or with your mom, your sister, or some other relative.

When He Has the Kids

Let's start with kids who live with your ex. Toward the end of this short chapter, we'll talk about kids who live with someone else.

Sometimes the courts decide it's best if the kids live with their father. Sometimes the two divorcing spouses agree between themselves that that's the better arrangement — "in the best interests of the children" is the phrase the courts like to use. Sometimes the arrangement is decided later on: The kids start out living with their mom but, after a while, for whatever reason, it's agreed that it would be better if the kids lived with their dad. Or the kids express a wish to live with Dad instead of Mom, and the parents agree to this arrangement.

There was a time when such a situation raised eyebrows universally. "What's wrong with her, that the court gave the father custody?" "What kind of mother is she, letting her ex-husband raise the kids?" Today, though a few eyebrows might still go up, more people tend to be accepting of this less-usual — yet increasingly common — custody arrangement.

In fact, there are plenty of reasons for the father being the logical choice of parent to have custody. To name just a few of the more obvious ones:

❖ The mother works long hours, or late hours, or a shift that has her out of the house while the kids are home, but the father works a shorter or more usual shift.

❖ The father has a home-based business and can be home for the kids even while he's working, while the mom works out of the house.

❖ The mom travels a lot on business. The dad does not.

❖ The mom has health problems.

❖ The mom has emotional or substance abuse issues.

❖ The kids are all boys, and old enough that the family agrees having their father around, a good male role model, may be more important for them than being with their mom.

❖ The dad has a strong desire to be the parent who raises the kids, promises to let the mom see them often, and she's comfortable with that arrangement.

The decision may be yours or the court's, and it may be one you're comfortable with, one you're unsure about, or one you're extremely unhappy about. Or it may be that *you're* all right with it, but you're wondering how the rest of the world will react. In fact, you may already be on the receiving end of some negative reactions.

Such criticism may come from family, friends, acquaintances, and even strangers, and may range from unbridled curiosity ("Why does your *ex* have the kids??!!") to shock, horror, and efforts to layer you with guilt. ("My dear, don't you think you have a responsibility to raise those kids yourself? After all, you *are* their mother!")

If you agreed to the arrangement, you might now begin to feel guilty. If the arrangement was settled by the court against your wishes, these comments will only deepen your resentment. If you're grieving because you don't have the kids living with you, such comments will only add to your burden. And if you're already feeling guilty because you're not raising the kids (whether the decision was one you agreed to or otherwise), such comments aren't going to help.

Let the Rest of the World Go By

How do you handle critical comments, well-meaning or simply rude, from people you're close to or those you hardly know? Try these answers on for size and see if one of them works for you:

❖ "Taking Tom's work schedule and mine into consideration, it really is best for the kids to live with him. I miss them, but I can't be selfish about it. I want to do what's best for them. "

❖ "Given how much I travel on business, I really thought it would be better for the kids to live with their dad instead of spending a lot of time with a baby sitter or being shunted back and forth between homes. After all, what's best for the kids is what's really most important, isn't it?"

❖ "I know Dick and I had our differences as a couple, but I never faulted him as a father. And the boys are at an age when they need a dad, a good strong role model, and that's Dick. This isn't about what I want. This is about what's best for the kids."

❖ "I won't lie to you. I wish I had them. It was the court's decision. There was a time when a mom had to really be unfit not to get custody. It's not like that anymore. The courts give dads custody a lot more readily now, and that's what happened here. But please don't make me feel any worse by dragging out the discussion. Let's talk about something else, OK?"

❖ "Lee decided he wanted to live with his dad, and Bryan and I talked it over and agreed it was a reasonable request for a boy to want to live with his male parent. We're both comfortable with it ... and, look, it's not set in stone. Lee could change his mind in time to come. But Bryan and I are working together and being flexible on this."

❖ "Keep in mind that I'm an ER nurse with lots of odd-hours shifts. It isn't really fair — or even safe — for the kids to be alone or in child care or with a sitter when they can be with their father and have a stable home life."

❖ "Doug lives in a better neighborhood in a better school district. I can't afford to move there, but if the kids live with Doug, they live in a safer area and go to better schools, so we're doing this for them."

❖ "We have our reasons. I really don't need to go into it. It's a decision we talked about long and hard, and we agreed mutually to do it this way. There are pros and cons, of course. Aren't there always? But in the balance, this seems the best decision, and we're sticking with it. I appreciate your respecting our decision."

There was a time when a mother would be universally derided if she put her career ahead of her kids, even if their father was willing to step into the breach and be a fully active parent. This applies in cases in which a married mom goes off to work and the dad stays home to raise the kids, and it applies in cases in which a divorced mom lets the dad have custody so she can more fully pursue her career.

There's certainly still a sizable segment of the population who believe that the mother should raise her kids...period! And if you voluntarily agree to your ex having custody, you do need to be prepared for some adverse opinions, whether they're expressed to your face or behind your back. But have the courage of your convictions and do what *you* believe is best for all concerned...for the kids and, yes, for you too, as long as you're content that your ex is giving the kids a good home and a good upbringing.

And what if you're *not* happy with the decision? What if you *aren't* okay with your ex having custody? You can fight him in court, and if the circumstances that led to the judge's decision change, or even if you go before a different judge, the outcome next time around might be different.

And meanwhile?

Meanwhile, stay in contact. Don't fume and fuss and tell the kids you're miserable, even if you are. Don't put them in the middle of the dispute if there is one. And don't put pressure on them by asking them to start a campaign to persuade Dad that they'd rather live with you. It's just not fair to them.

Let them know that you love them, that you think about them when they're not around, that you miss them, and that you value the time you spend with them. (You should do this whether or not you're happy with the decision for them to live with their dad!)

Be faithful to the visitation schedule. Be there on time. Be prepared to spend "quality time" with them when they're with you.

Prove Your Love by Being With Them, and Being You

"Uncle Daddy, the Ice Cream Man," aka "Disneyland Dad" has already made an appearance in this book. You may remember that we labeled his female counterpart as "Mall Mom," also known as "Mama Softouch." These are the parents who try to express their love to their children through money, goodies, and carnival rides.

Don't fall into the Mall/Softouch trap. Don't try to prove to the kids how much you love them by taking them on frequent, extravagant shopping trips and buying them whatever they want, even if you can afford to. This proves only that you can be manipulated through guilt. *Do* prove your love by visiting them as often as you can, asking interested questions about their lives, really listening when they talk to you, giving good and caring advice when they ask, supporting their activities however you can, and doing fun things with them when you're together.

"Fun things" does not necessarily mean taking them to an amusement park or spending way beyond your budget on a trip to the video arcade. Of course, you can do that once in a while if it's within your budget, but cooking with them is fun, too. Reading to them — or with them — is fun. Going to the playground, playing catch, or helping them with their sports skills — even if you're only halfway good at the sport — can be great fun. If your kids have collections — coins, stamps, dolls, model rockets, antique toys — take them to a coin or stamp show, a doll exhibit, or some other event themed to their hobbies or interests. How about forming a family singing group or band, or just making music together for fun?

Most communities have at least one theater company offering children's theater, and if the kids are young, a local production of *Once Upon a Mattress, The Three Little Pigs,* or another children's play should be an affordable outing for you all. If they're older, consider going to the latest *Star Wars* or *Harry Potter* movie. Or rent a couple of age-appropriate videos or DVDs and explode some popcorn in your microwave.

How about a ball game, concert, or community festival? Almost every town has an annual Fourth of July picnic or parade, Founder's Day celebration, or something related to the local heritage or industry, such as a strawberry festival, German Days, or Cinco de Mayo. Sports fans don't have to travel far these days to take in professional or semi-pro games, and the local college or high school teams are likely to offer an exciting afternoon or evening of action, with something fun for almost everyone.

A day at the beach or lake, a hike or bike ride, an overnight campout (even if it's in your own backyard) can be a memorable, fun, and affordable experience.

Be there for them. Don't limit yourself solely to passive entertainment. Be there to talk, to have fun, to be serious. Draw with little ones, or tell them stories. Play video games with older ones, or ask them about school. (Emphasize the fun stuff!) Talk to them at any age — about their lives, their concerns, the fun things they've done since they saw you last, their friends, the questions they might want answered, and the projects they're working on.

Make your time together creative fun. Play boxed games, or card games, or old-fashioned games that don't come in boxes — hide 'n' seek, or catch, or kick the can, or capture the flag, or any of the other classics. Create games with them, centered around things they know about. If they're older and interested, help them to explore the wider world: science (with chemistry sets or telescopes); art (visit a gallery or museum or show, or set up an easel or pottery bench and do it together!); nature (with a walk on the beach or a hike in the mountains); politics (watch the United States Congress on C-Span, or take in a school board or city council meeting, or just talk about current events).

There are tons of ways to spend loving, creative, fun, memorable time with your children, even if the visits are short and only occasional. Do remember that they won't be children long. Make the most of every day.

Are They with Someone Else?

What about kids who live neither with you nor with your ex, but with another family member — your mom, your sister, your former sister-in-law...? Rarely is such an arrangement mandated by the court. It is almost always entered into by mutual agreement of the parents.

Why does such an arrangement occur?

Often it's a question of the mother feeling that either her work schedule or her emotional state doesn't give her the latitude to be the best of all possible mothers. It may be that you're still in college — or you're back to school after time off to raise your young children — and you aren't as available to your kids as you'd like to be. Or your work schedule is such that you can't physically be there for the kids when they need you. It may be that emotionally you just don't feel prepared to cope single-handedly, without a husband backing you up. And perhaps you'd rather see them raised by another woman than by your ex, or perhaps your ex himself is not willing or able to undertake raising the kids.

We want to say here, unequivocally, that there is no shame in this. The only shame is in trying to brave it out when there is help available and you're too proud to take it. If you can't make it on your own, but have no one to turn to, of course you'll do everything you can to give them the best life possible. But the best opportunity for the children may be with your mom, sister, former sister-in-law, or another reliable, responsible adult who wants to take the kids in. If you just can't do it all on your own, for whatever reasons, and you have that option, do consider it seriously.

It is not a sign of weakness or a fault or failure in you to recognize that you're not able to do the best possible job of raising your kids by yourself, and instead to accept help from another trusted family member.

Of course, if you are truly not content that the person offering to help can do a good job and raise the kids the way you want them raised, the story changes. If you fear that your mom, sister, or whoever will raise your kids with values you're not happy with, or in any other way that's not comfortable for you, keep searching for other options.

Get some help with this very important decision if you're not sure what to do. Check with your local independent Family Services Center, a pastoral counselor, or perhaps a professional child psychologist or other therapist, to help you sort out the issues. Don't, however, rush to the local "department of children and families" or "child welfare services." You don't want to put your children into "the system" unless you have exhausted all the other possibilities.

Your first and only concern should be *what's best for the kids*. Not what the neighbors will say. Not what will float along the gossip grapevine. Not the guilt trip family or friends or society tries to lay on you.

What we've said about visiting the kids if they live with your ex holds true in these circumstances too, of course. See them as often as you can. Talk to them about fun stuff, about life, about love, and about things that are important to them and things that are important to you. Send them e-mail notes between visits. Call them on the phone. Let them know you're there for them. Let them know you miss them when you're not with them.

A Caveat or Two

As you examine the possibilities for involving your extended family or friends in caring for your children, remember that there may be limits on what you are permitted to do under the court's parenting order. Consider these factors:

❖ Your ex probably will need to agree to any arrangements you make for anything beyond "normal day care."

❖ Be very careful not to make any arrangements — even "informally" — that might jeopardize your custody. If the court said the children are to live with you, that's where they'd better be living.

❖ Are there restrictions on where you and the children may live? (For example, you may not be allowed to move out of the state without the court's permission.)

❖ You might want to consult your divorce attorney or a licensed mental health professional (psychologist, marriage and family therapist, clinical social worker) who's a specialist in custody matters. Some specialists go under various other titles, such as "custody evaluator," or "special master," or "divorce mediator," or "parenting coordinator." Choose carefully, on recommendation from trusted sources.

❖ Even if all the legal hurdles are cleared, we suggest you consider a formal agreement with the caregiver — even if it's your mom — spelling out lots of the details. Take a look at the outline for a "parenting plan" at the end of chapter 12 for ideas.

You'll Always Be Their Mom

You're still their mother. It's not carved in stone that a mother has to be the person who rears her children. A mother is someone who puts the best interests of her kids above everything else. Do you love them enough to let someone else raise them, if that someone is in a position to do a better job than you currently are? That's a way of showing love too, you know, when you love them enough to let someone else raise them — if doing so is the best thing *for the kids.*

Sure you want them with you, but putting their well-being above your own desires is real love, and don't let anyone tell you otherwise!

AfterWords — Chapter Nine

Key Points in the Chapter

- There are many good reasons why your children might live with their father. There's no need to be embarrassed if that's your family situation.

- Respond assertively to those who are critical of your family structure. "We've worked out an arrangement that we consider best for our kids."

- The best way to prove your love for your children is to be present in their lives, not to be the big spender who gives them everything they want. Lots of wonderful family activities cost virtually nothing. Time with you is priceless.

- In many families, the best arrangement is for a trusted family member to care for the children.

- Be sure any child care arrangement you make is permissible under the court-approved parenting plan.

Activity of the Week

- If your children don't live with you (or even if they do!), plan a special visit that costs virtually nothing. Stay overnight at a public campground. Shop together for a picnic in the park or at the beach. Visit a favorite — or new-to-you — museum. Go to the library and explore topics together among the shelves. Go to a free or low-cost concert, or ball game, or play. Take a hike. Ride bikes (rent a tandem?). Fly kites. Get your favorite instruments out and play music together. Whatever you do, put the emphasis on being together, talking, being a family — not on shopping or spending!

Suggested Readings and Resources

Lansky, V. (1989). *Vicki Lansky's Divorce Book for Parents: Helping Your Children Cope With Divorce And Its Aftermath.* New York: Signet Books.

Ricci, I. (1980). *Mom's House, Dad's House: Making Shared Custody Work.* New York: Macmillan Publishing Co.

Rofes, E. (editor) (1981). *The Kids' Book Of Divorce: By, For & About Kids.* New York: Vintage Books.

Stahl, P. (2000). *Parenting After Divorce.* Atascadero, CA: Impact Publishers.

10

· · · · · · · · · ·

If Your "Kids" Aren't Kids Any More

Not every divorced woman has young kids, but if your kids are grown and on their own, that doesn't guarantee fewer problems related to the divorce.

Grown kids can offer some major hassles. Other relatives, and even friends, can also offer a share of problems. But at least their words don't normally carry as much weight, and failing all else, you can cease talking to them till they get the message and stop interfering and causing problems. But that's not an easy option with your adult kids.

Can They Save the Marriage?

While younger kids are more forcefully impacted by a divorce than are kids who no longer live in your home, grown kids are affected in their own way...and are more able to speak up to you about the divorce and even to take active steps to try to counter it.

Ashley and Curtis's marriage was a casualty of mid-life changes — his more so than hers. Both partners grew restless as middle age descended on them, the kids left home, and they faced the perennial question: What now?

Ashley's discontent resulted in a change of hair color and style and a mini face-lift. She quit her job to "follow her bliss" and open a small antiques store. Curtis, not to be outdone, began an affair with a neighbor.

In a scene right out of a bad novel, Ashley closed the store early on Curtis's birthday and came home to make him a surprise dinner...only to get a surprise herself when she found her husband was home already — and in bed with the neighbor.

Contrary to what you might expect, that wasn't the immediate cause of the divorce. There was a scene, of course, and Curtis spent about a month sleeping in the guest room. Ashley demanded that Curtis give up the relationship with the neighbor "and anyone else you're running around with," but she didn't ask for a divorce.

It was Curtis who did that, about two months later. He said that he felt that Ashley no longer trusted him (which was true), that he couldn't live like that, and that he wanted a divorce.

Ashley countered with the suggestion that they seek marriage counseling, that maybe she could learn to trust him again if she felt he was addressing the root of the problem. She still loved him, she said, and she didn't want a divorce. She just didn't want him cheating on her.

But Curtis had been feeling penned in for the last two months, with no intimacy with Ashley, no extramarital pleasures, and no prospect of resuming them. The idea of spending the rest of his life with Ashley alone sent him into a tailspin. He was convinced there was something better out there, and he didn't want to be cheated out of his chance to find it. No, he said, he didn't want to go into counseling…he wanted a divorce. He wasn't getting any younger, and he wanted to have "some fun."

When he first moved out, Ashley tried to get him back. The lines of communication were still open, and she did her best to tempt him back into the marriage. But after a couple of months, and with Curtis resolute, hiring a lawyer, and serving Ashley with papers, her own feelings changed. She began to realize she could never be comfortable with Curtis or trust him again, and maybe a divorce *was* the best thing.

Their only child, Todd, lived close by, but at first they managed to keep him from finding out what was happening. Eventually, of course, he had to be told. Todd was up in arms when he learned of his parents' impending divorce, and he did everything he could think of to try to impede it.

Even after the divorce became final, Todd's every phone call to either parent included some sort of maneuver to get them back together. And when verbally hounding them didn't work, Todd moved to "Plan B" — getting them both in the same room in hopes it would lead to reconciliation. He invited each of them over for drinks at his house, "and then we'll go out to dinner," but he didn't tell either one that the other was coming.

The plan backfired in more ways than one. In what was unquestionably a display of bad manners under any circumstances, Curtis brought an uninvited and unannounced guest…his latest girlfriend. So not only were Curtis and Ashley thrown together unwittingly, but the presence of Janis, the girlfriend, set the tensions on high for everyone.

Ashley finished her drink hastily and excused herself with "Maybe this isn't a good night for us to have dinner. Let me take a raincheck." Janis, finding herself in the unhappy middle of a family drama, asked Curtis to please take her home. And Curtis, who was as much to blame as Todd, tried to heap all the blame onto Todd for inviting Curtis and Ashley both without either of them knowing the other was coming. In his attempt to shift any blame away from himself, Curtis created a big scene before taking Janis — by now thoroughly mortified — home.

In the aftermath — peppered with recriminating phone calls and angry conversations among all the parties — Ashley blamed Todd as much as she blamed Curtis. Had Todd not attempted to sneakily maneuver his parents together, the whole awkward scene would never have occurred.

The relationship was strained between Todd and his parents for several months thereafter, although even that didn't stop Todd from making occasional suggestions that Curtis and Ashley get back together!

Adult kids can be very distressed when their parents divorce, and because they're grown, they sometimes feel they can take matters into their own hands and try to head off the divorce or even re-cement the couple after the decree is final.

Similarly, the parents of the divorcing couple can interfere if they are distressed at their grown child's divorce, or if they feel they still know what's best for their child.

Can You Reason With Them?

Sometimes explaining the circumstances behind the divorce will elicit greater understanding, but that's a questionable tack to take where your adult kids are concerned. If your husband was unfaithful or abusive, for example, your kids might be more sympathetic to the divorce if they knew the facts. But do you really want to tell them, "Dad was cheating on me" or "Dad hit me" or "Dad was emotionally/verbally abusive"? After all, he's still their father and they still love him. While you don't want them hassling you to return to him, or maneuvering to get the two of you back together, or thinking ill of you for leaving him (because they don't know the reason), tearing him down in their eyes is not a great choice either.

What to say then? Consider something like this: "There are things you don't know. And frankly, I don't plan to tell you. Your father is still your father. What went wrong is between him and me. I have no need to bad-mouth him to his own kids. You'll just have to take my word that I had good and ample reason for leaving him, and let it go at that. But he's still your father, and I want you still to love and respect him. So I won't say any more. But please respect *me* too, and understand that I had my reasons for leaving him."

And if *he* left *you* but the damage is done and you no longer want him back? "You may be an adult now, but your father and I are still entitled to our privacy. There are some things we don't care to share. The marriage is over; that's the way it is. We're both okay with the decision, and you need to respect it. You don't have to agree with everything we do, or know the reasons for it, but we do ask you to respect our decisions."

Even if your husband was the one who asked for the divorce, and you'd still like him back if only it were possible, your adult children are only rubbing a raw wound by urging you to reconcile with him. Surely you've suggested marital counseling, asked him to reconsider, tried to work out your problems. If none of that worked, there's nothing they can say that will help or make a difference. They're "preaching to the choir," and they're only making you feel worse.

Even if they, like Todd, invite you to dinner together to "try to talk things out," or suggest the name of that great marriage counselor who helped cousin Andrew, it's not going to help. You tried counseling, to no avail. Or you suggested it, but he wasn't having any. The sooner they accept the divorce as reality, the easier it will be for you to heal...a point you should definitely make in your conversations with them.

What of adult kids who take sides? We hope your grown kids won't take sides...nor should you expect or encourage them to. It's not appropriate for you to recite a litany of their father's faults, either to justify your having left him or to evoke the kids' partisan sympathies. Even if your ex tells them, in an effort to elicit their sympathies to his cause, a false version of why he left you or why you left him, you can say, "That's *his* version," or "That's not the whole truth," without reciting to them the full gospel according to Mom. Keep it factual — as you see it — and be straight with them. Think of it as similar to the way you told them about sex when they were small: just answer their questions factually, and don't tell them more than they need — or are ready — to hear. The full story will likely come out over time.

Marriages End for Lots of Reasons

Of course, sometimes there *are* no serious misdeeds on either side. Some marriages fall apart without either spouse doing anything seriously wrong to the other. Sometimes, when the kids are grown and gone, the couple realizes that the kids were really all that held them together. Now, without any kids in the house, they have nothing in common, no common goals or interest, and no real love. The marriage sputters and dies.

And of course there are marriages that had fallen apart years earlier, in which the couple realizes they are mismatched and ill-suited, but stay together just for the sake of the kids. Once the kids are gone, there is no further reason to keep together a marriage that is not happy for either spouse.

Some marriages simply fall prey to middle-age restlessness, even if that restlessness doesn't result in either partner straying. But one spouse or the other feels unfulfilled and, feeling the grip of middle age, wants to strike out and "find real happiness before it's too late."

All these are harder to explain satisfactorily to the kids, even though there's less reason to maintain secrecy. When there's no blame, no finger-pointing, no "It's all his fault — it's because of what he did," there's less need to keep it from the (grown) kids. "Your father and I just don't love each other anymore" is pretty neutral, and there's no reason you need to avoid saying it to your grown children. But it will be harder for them to understand. You used to love each other. You've been married so many years now. You didn't do anything bad to him. He didn't do anything bad to you. How could you just stop loving each other?

Bear in mind that this not only disturbs them on the obvious level but also, whether or not they realize it, on a deeper level: If Mom and Dad could fall out of love for no good reason after all these years, who's to say their own marriages are safe and sacrosanct? Might the same thing happen to them? Could it be in the genes?

"I Don't Want to Talk About It"

On the other hand, there are kids who don't want to hear *anything* about the divorce. Not even the problems you're having now as a result of the divorce or of living alone. "That was your choice,

Mom," they'll say, whether you left your husband or he left you. Their attitude is, "You made your bed, now lie in it," and when you try to tell them that you're lonely, or pinched for money, or feeling lost, they don't want to hear it.

This may arise from a judgmental attitude, or it may just be their inability to cope. They may be shutting you down because they can't deal with knowing their mom is in trouble. Before you criticize them for a callous, hard-headed attitude, stop and consider whether it might be a case of their being unable to handle your pain.

Even as adults, it's tough to see our moms hurting.

Can't We All Just Get Along?

Your adult children may take the divorce in stride. They certainly understand that it's not uncommon in society today. They may even have seen it coming over the years. Or, on the other hand, they may be unable to tolerate that the adults they've always depended upon have broken up the only family they've known. They may react emotionally and blow up at both of you. Whatever their response to the divorce, they need the same reassurance younger children require. Mom and Dad will always love them, and the divorce was in no way their fault.

Who knows? You may be better friends now that they can relate to you as an independent adult. And friendship with an adult child is something to treasure and hold dear.

AfterWords — Chapter Ten

Key Points in the Chapter

- Even grown children may try to prevent their parents' divorce.

- Children — of any age — are not entitled to know all the details of their parents' divorce. Some things are between you and your ex alone. You can be honest with your children without telling them all the details.

- The choice of how much to tell your children is always yours.

- Adult children — just like youngsters — need reassurance that their parents will always love them, and that the divorce was not their fault.

Activity of the Week

- Write a letter to each of your adult children — even if they live near you — and tell them whatever you want them to know about the divorce. Again, keep to yourself those details you don't want to share with them. Your goal is to be sure they are not misinformed about what happened to your marriage — as you see it. After you've written the letter(s), you may decide not to mail it (them).

Suggested Readings and Resources

Lewis, J.M. and Blakeslee, S. (2003). *The Unexpected Legacy of Divorce.* New York: Hyperion.

Wenning, K. (1998). *Men Are from Earth, Women Are from Earth.* New York: Jason Aronson.

Zimmerman, J. and Thayer, E. (2003). *Adult Children of Divorce.* Oakland, CA: New Harbinger.

After Your Divorce

PART FOUR

Adults in Your Life

11

• • • • • • • • • •

About Your Family and Friends

FAMILY AND FRIENDS. The people who should be your allies, your support network, your safety net. And in most cases they will be. In most cases...

Think for a moment about those anxious times when...

... you're not sure you did the right thing in leaving him, or

... you still don't know why he left you, or

... you know you made the right move but, dammit, it's tough being on your own again, or

... you're really uptight because the money's not going to make it to the end of the month, or

... you ran into him at the bank yesterday and got "all shook up" about it.

When any of these, or a myriad of other situations, has you blue, angry, or coming unhinged, you need a trusted shoulder to cry on (both figuratively and literally).

Sometimes you need advice; most often you just need someone to listen — usually a close female friend or relative (your sister, your mom, your favorite aunt). Or it could be a male friend or relative, who can help you see things from a guy's perspective. Usually those closest to you are good choices. Usually, but not always.

Parents Will Be Parents

Your parents, of course, are expected to take your side, no matter how fond they were of their son-in-law. Nevertheless, sometimes the parents of a divorcing woman are concerned that she's not going to be able to make it on her own — financially, emotionally, or practically (such as in the matter of raising her kids without a husband around the house to help). Sometimes, too, the parents of the divorced or divorcing woman have more selfish motives at heart: They fear that she will move back in with them and/or rely on them for financial aid once she no longer has a husband, and they're unready, or unable, to be thrust into that position.

Religion often plays a part in the objections of parents as well. Catholics in particular, and certain Protestant denominations as well, view marriage as a lifelong commitment and divorce as impermissible. If you've crossed that line, you're considered a serious sinner and — despite the concept of forgiveness that goes with these belief systems — that breach can be very difficult for parents to tolerate. (In fairness, however, it should be noted that the popular Rebuilding divorce seminars developed by Dr. Bruce Fisher are often sponsored by churches — including Catholic parishes.)

If your parents are giving you problems, bear in mind that they have your welfare and happiness at heart. It will be hard for them to hear, but something like this must be said: "Mom, Dad, I'm a grown woman. I know what's best for me. I know we're a close family, but there are some things about the marriage that I haven't discussed with you, and that's the way it's going to stay. You're just going to have to trust that I've made the best decision for myself. Now, you're not helping me any by bringing it up over and over. I'm not going back to him, I've done the best thing, and it's not open for discussion. If you don't get off the topic, I'm going to wind up cutting back on my visits to you. You don't allow me to be happy or comfortable when you keep bringing it up. The divorce is a reality you need to accept. Now drop it and let's move on."

Don't You Wish — Sometimes — They'd Just Leave You Alone?

Isn't there always one friend, or one relative, or possibly several of each, with whom you wish you didn't have to discuss the divorce at all? You may know better than to ask your Aunt Amy for advice, or to tell your friend Mia that you're feeling kind of down. But that won't stop them from offering unsolicited advice or comments anyhow. And you can hardly keep the fact of the divorce from them altogether!

What are some of the things that people — well-intentioned and otherwise — will say and do that are unhelpful, even painful?

❖ They'll tell you horror stories from their own divorces (or those of their friends) when what you really need is cheering up, not a recitation of how much worse it might get.

❖ They'll try to lay a guilt trip on you over leaving your husband (or letting him leave) instead of "trying harder to make it work."

❖ They'll try to lay a guilt trip on you over what the divorce is doing to your kids.

❖ They'll give you advice that you know is all wrong for you, and be hurt or miffed when you don't follow it.

❖ They'll tell you that, since you were the one who initiated the divorce, you're getting no sympathy from them. This is all *your* doing.

❖ They'll "dig for dirt" and want to know *why* the divorce occurred, even though the person asking is *not* one of your close friends, and you don't feel like "washing your dirty laundry in public."

❖ They'll try to start a pity party — "Oh, poor you!" — when you're working hard to convince yourself that you're doing fine, and are beginning to be at least halfway successful in this process.

Some of these "friends" focus attention on your ex, and what's going on with him these days. Their motives may be innocent, mischievous, or malevolent:

❖ They're simply gossips who love to spread a "good" story. Or they hope that by feeding you some "juicy morsels" on your ex, you'll return with some more hot gossip.

❖ They're people who lead dull lives and like to stir up excitement in other people's lives and then sit back and watch the fireworks. It's more exciting than television.

❖ They want to help you, and they mistakenly think that giving you reports on the actions of your ex is helpful.

❖ They think it's great that you're finally divorced, they want to make sure you stay that way, and so they give you reports on the worst behaviors and actions of your ex to keep your anger stirred up.

❖ They think it's terrible that you're divorced, they'd love to see you two reunited, and so they give you (and possibly him, too!) reports designed to pull you back together.

These people love to feed you information—whether old or recent — about your ex. It may precede the divorce: "Do you know that, while you two were still married, I saw Ed kiss some woman in the bank parking lot? I don't know who she was, but Ed sure seemed to know her pretty well!" Or it may be as current as the eleven o'clock news: "Do you know Ed *still* isn't dating anyone? I know for a fact that he sits home alone every night except for Wednesday night bowling league and his Friday night poker game."

The information they feed you may be truth, half-truth, completely bogus, or wild speculation.

The information may be intended to make you feel more kindly toward your ex, dispose you to like him even less than before, or simply make you regard the friend who's telling you the story as valuable because she keeps you informed.

The best way to handle such information is to stop it before it starts. "Thank you, but I'd really rather not discuss my ex-husband. What else do we have to talk about?" Of course, you're going to discuss him with your best friend; you have to spill your feelings and get advice when you need it from someone. Confine your conversations to one or two or three close friends, and be sure these are people who can be counted on to give accurate, untainted, unbiased feedback.

Self-Defense When Dealing with "Buttinskis"

Have we covered all the things people do wrong, albeit with (most of the time) the best of intentions? Probably not, but let's turn our attention to what you can do in self-defense when you're facing a "buttinski"?

❖ Don't bring up the subject of your divorce unnecessarily with anyone you're not confident will give you a helpful, or at least neutral, response. And if you must bring it up? Suppose someone you don't see often runs into you in the supermarket and asks, "How's your hubby?" or the mother of a friend of your child calls up and, not knowing of the divorce, asks if you, your now-ex-husband, and your two kids can come over to her child's birthday barbeque? In the first case, "I'm sure Andy's doing well, but he's not my husband anymore." In the second example, "Well, Bryan and I aren't married any longer, but the kids and I would love to come to the barbeque, if that still fits your plans." The appropriate response by the person doing the inquiry is simply, "Oh, I'm sorry," or "Sorry to hear it." At that point, all you need to say is, "Thank you," and then change the subject. This signals that you are not open for a discussion of what happened, or of anything else relevant to the divorce.

❖ Don't complain to anyone you know is likely to give bad advice. (What worked for your friend Sheila may have been great for her but wouldn't work for you. Different people, different circumstances, despite some similarities in the situation. If you think Sheila won't realize this, don't complain to her. If she asks how you're handling things post-divorce, you can say, "I'm coping." This implies that it isn't easy but you're managing. It also signals that you don't want advice, especially if you deflect further conversation on the topic by asking her a question on a totally different subject.)

❖ If someone asks a question you don't want to answer, or offers advice or commentary you don't want to hear, put up your hand in a "Stop" motion (unless you're talking by phone, of course!) and say, "Wait. Please. I really don't want to discuss this. Let's talk about something other than my divorce." Say it firmly. And be ready with an alternative subject, whether it's "Did I tell you my sister just got an award at work?" or "How are your tomato plants coming along?" or "Can you believe the latest polls in the campaign for mayor?" By pre-emptively switching the subject, you forestall, "But I just want to tell you ..." or "I only wanted to know if...."

❖ If someone tries to opine that you made a mistake in divorcing your husband or letting him divorce you, say, "I realize it may seem that way to someone who doesn't know the whole story, but things often aren't what they seem. I don't want to go into the subject any further, so that's where we'll have to leave it." You might add, "I'll appreciate it if we can talk about something else now."

❖ If they try to compare your situation with their own (or their friend's or cousin's or neighbor's) horrible divorce, and paint a very bleak picture, you can always say, "Well, fortunately the circumstances aren't quite the same. So I hope things will be different for me! Now, let's talk about something more cheerful."

❖ And if they try to start a pity party, tell them forthrightly, "I need cheering up, not depressing. I don't *want* to sit here feeling sorry for myself. Now, got any good news to share with me? What's good in *your* life that you can tell me about?"

❖ If they try to give you unwanted advice, or advice that you know is wrong for you, try this: "That may be good advice in some similar circumstances, but it doesn't exactly fit my situation. Thanks for trying to help, but I'll have to figure it out." Then change the subject.

❖ If they tell you that you'll get no sympathy from them because you were the one who initiated the divorce, reply along the lines of, "I wasn't looking for sympathy. I was just stating the facts. Please don't judge me. You don't know all the facts, and I don't want to talk about them."

❖ If they snoop and dig for dirt, say, "I may be going through a rough patch, but I don't need to air my dirty laundry in public. This is between me and Karl."

Where Did All Those "Friends" Go, Anyway?

Just when you most need your friends, of course, some of them may become "unavailable" — often scared off by the divorce. And you yourself may pull uncomfortably back from others.

Who are your closest friends? Did you, during your marriage, still have some friends who were single, or who were married but socialized with you primarily one-on-one, rather than couple-and-couple? Particularly if you retained your career after you married, you likely have some friends from work, as well as perhaps friends from your single days who remained single, or whose husbands never became friends with your husband. At least one or two of these are probably people with whom you now feel comfortable talking frankly about the divorce and about your current situation in the aftermath.

On the other hand, it's likely that most of your friends are one-half of a couple that you and your husband socialized with together. And you may not be as comfortable talking with them or socializing with them now. If you have dinner with the couple, you'll be on pins and needles knowing anything you say in front of the husband is likely to get back to your ex. And you'll be uncomfortable knowing the husband that you're socializing with is probably sitting in judgment of you for the divorce, regardless of who initiated it. It's only natural for him to stick up for another male. (Of course, this won't *always* be the case, but often enough it is.) Even if you meet with the wife alone, will you be comfortable talking to her frankly and openly? Or will you hold back, knowing she might repeat some of the conversation to her husband, who might then say something to your ex?

Apart from the issue of having to monitor yourself for what you say that might get back to your ex, will you be emotionally comfortable socializing with other couples? Many women feel awkward socializing solo with a twosome, whether or not they're friends from couple days. And for a woman who's lonely or otherwise unhappy to no longer be half of a couple, socializing with a duo can make her acutely more aware of her solo status.

Unfortunately, many women, once they get married, gravitate to friendships with other couples and drop — or put on the back burner — their friendships with single women (or women whose husbands don't relate well to the woman's husband). Even women who continue to work and form office friendships may not get close with these friends from work and may not feel they want to suddenly start socializing with them — or pouring out their woes to them — in the wake of a divorce.

You Need Friends!

Don't hibernate! You need friends for a variety of reasons. Here are a few notable ones:

❖ To have compatible adults to spend time with, which is always necessary, but more so in the absence of that adult relationship that has just ended.

❖ To have people to whom you can comfortably express your feelings about your present situation. These feelings will change as you go through the various stages post-divorce and the various experiences that are likely to occur. Recall some of the "rebuilding block" feelings discussed in chapter 2: denial, fear, loneliness, guilt, grief, anger.

❖ To have someone who'll listen as you share your frustration that there aren't enough hours in the day now that you have to do it all yourself.

❖ For non-emotional reasons: trading childcare; sharing rides; getting advice on shopping for bargains; borrowing tools; finding a mechanic or plumber; helping with a Cub Scout dinner; advancing ten dollars till payday.

Whatever it is you're feeling, you need a friend, whether you want advice, a sounding board, or simply a sympathetic ear.

You need to recognize the emotional need to have friends, friends with whom you can express your feelings and from whom you can get trustworthy advice. That need is important for your emotional well-being. Recognize and respect your need to talk to friends. Don't keep your emotions and your problems, including those of a more practical nature, bottled up inside you. And if you don't have friends you're comfortable spilling to, as well as friends whose advice you respect, you need to work on finding new friends.

Don't Throw Away Your Old Friends

Whatever discomfort you feel about talking openly in front of your ex-husband's friends, that doesn't mean you need to discard all your old friends. If you're no longer comfortable socializing with Sheila and Derek, you can still socialize with Sheila. And in time, when you're feeling less pained about being on your own, you may well be comfortable having dinners with the two of them again. For now, though, stay close with Sheila if that works for you. Meet her for lunch, jogging, shared manicure appointments, and other things you can do together as just the two of you — and maybe sometimes the two of you and your respective kids.

Perhaps you'll be comfortable talking openly with her when her husband's not around. And if you're loath to discuss anything that might get from Sheila to Derek to your ex, even though Derek's not present, there are plenty of other things to talk about. The divorce, events in your life in the wake of it, and your feelings about all these things may be the most important topics in your life right now, but surely there are other things going on in your life as well. So talk to Sheila and your other friends about other topics. Discuss your job, your kids, your parents, your sister, the state of world affairs, the upcoming local elections, the way you caught your auto mechanic overcharging you, the new art display in the library lobby, the latest new movie.

The divorce need not — and should not — be your only topic of conversation.

Divorce in Uniform

In a category of their own are military wives, whose husbands' careers provide many a minefield for a marriage. During the early years of the Iraq War (2003–2005), for instance, the U.S. Army reported that its divorce rate jumped more than 80 percent.

When one spouse is deployed long-term, and therefore living apart from the other, the situation is rife with opportunities for problems. Under such circumstances, maintaining fidelity (on both sides!) is often an issue. Whether it's the husband who wanders or the wife, the result is often divorce.

Most left-behind spouses don't cheat at all, but many do feel the need for more contact than their deployed partners are able to provide. Wanting the companionship, emotional support, parenting help, and physical presence unavailable in a long-distance relationship, some opt to divorce and look elsewhere rather than do without — or go astray.

For a military wife, her husband's absence because of deployment is not the only problem, of course. Life in the military is often a series of moves, with the service member being transferred from base to base to base. Not every wife can easily handle being uprooted, torn from her friends, and forced to start over every couple of years. She must cope with missing old friends, meeting new people, learning her way around a new base and a new town, transferring her kids into new schools, adapting to a new climate, and all the other stressors that accompany a move.

The physical environment alone offers significant challenges. Consider the change of clothing, housing, and lifestyle in a move from Elmendorf Air Force Base in Alaska to Hickam Air Force Base in Hawaii! Or from part-time national guard service at Camp Grafton, North Dakota, in the northern plains to active duty at Fort Polk, Louisiana, on the Gulf Coast. And what about the Navy wife who has just made friends and bought summery outfits for a tour in San Diego when the Navy says, "You're off to Portsmouth, New Hampshire!"

Always wondering if a soldier will be sent into harm's way is enough to have caused many military spouses to throw up their hands and give up on the marriage.

Then there is the regimentation of the armed forces, an attitude that many service members carry over into their private lives. The freewheeling, laid back, and casual woman who marries a member of one of the armed services may chafe as he becomes increasingly by-the-book at home. And while the old adage posits that opposites attract, attracting is one thing; living together in harmony is something quite different.

Too, a service member's pay is not comparable to the average civilian's, a situation that naturally impacts on the spouse and children. Interestingly, however, military pay and benefits favor married personnel over singles, thus encouraging marriage at an age and life situation when it might not be the best of alternatives.

The vast majority of military careers begin early in life, of course, so there is a greater tendency for early marriages than in the general population. In fact, one recent study shows that for the population under twenty, while just one percent of civilians are married, nearly 14 percent of military members are! Marrying too young, together with the other stresses we've discussed here, contributes to a much higher rate of failed marriages among military couples.

As if these factors didn't make it tough enough on military marriages, there is yet another that can be the final straw. If husband and wife live apart for months at a time, she may discover that she can get along perfectly well on her own. After all, hasn't she been taking care of the kids, balancing the checkbook, and mowing the lawn by herself, anyway? What does she need him for? What may be bad for the marriage is not necessarily bad for the individual partners.

If you're a woman whose ex-husband is in the armed forces, you may have divorced because of one of these factors or some other situation directly related to his membership in the service. Now that you're on your own again, who are your friends? With whom can you discuss the stresses and disappointments that led to your military divorce? The people who could understand best would be other military wives...but now that you're out of the marriage, you're also off the base, no longer living among those who know the territory.

Your family and friends in the civilian world offer a vital source of comfort and companionship, of course. Your situation as a newly divorced woman largely parallels the situation of many other divorced women — whether their exes were soldiers, dentists, or librarians — and the many ideas and suggestions we've offered in this book apply to you. But don't neglect to reach out — by phone, letters, email, visits — to your former military-spouse neighbors and friends who understand what you went through. The road that led to your divorce is one that may best be understood by other military wives. Be sure to include them in your support circle.

Are You Wearing Your Divorce on Your Sleeve?

While we're on the subject of spilling to friends, let's talk briefly about women who "cry" on *all* their friends' shoulders. (Not you, right?) Such women are usually looking for sympathy, but the complaints get old fast, and they alienate their friends. Especially when word gets around that the woman is using everyone's shoulder for a crying towel.

If she's known to be a chronic complainer, friends will start avoiding her after a while. Seeing her number on the caller ID, they'll let it ring into voicemail. Then they'll call back just before it's time to pick up the kids from scouts or band practice: "I only have five minutes, but I wanted to return your call." (Translation: "I didn't want to return your call, so I called you when I had only five minutes.")

Such women often wind up getting conflicting advice, which can only confuse them further. While many women understand that a woman who's complaining may only want a shoulder and not advice, some will give advice even when it's not really wanted. And others, hearing continual griping, feel that if the complainer cannot get a grip, she *needs* advice to help pull her life together — whether she's asking for help or not. But six different friends are likely to offer just as many different opinions.

Now what is she to do? Listen to Ellen, Alison, Liz, or Saundra? It's confusing; too much advice can be worse than none. And if she decides Liz's advice sounds best for her, Alison and Ellen and Saundra are likely to get their feelings hurt — which may impact on the tenor of their friendships with her.

And of course, the more friends she complains to, the more likely it is that some of what she's saying — or a distorted version thereof — will get back to her ex-husband. Now, there are some women who *want* exactly that to happen. Hubby was the one who left, and the wife wants him to feel guilty, so she spreads her misery far and wide, hoping word will get back to him. They think guilt might drive him back home. Even if he doesn't come home, however, he'll stew in his own guilt...and the S.O.B. deserves it! (Or so their thinking goes.)

Reality check: That's a game. Don't play games. If you want him back, make a straightforward attempt to attain that goal. If you rope him back through guilt, he'll only resent you, and you'll have all your previous marital problems *plus* a heavy load of resentment. *Not* a solid foundation for a revitalized marriage!

Brighter Days with Family and Friends

If you've spent some time alone, without any close personal relationships, it can be easy to look for a new romance to fill your emotional gaps. As we've pointed out before, this is not the time to do that. Better that you work at finding and developing new friendships, visit a long-neglected cousin, or work at renewing your relationship with Mom. Plenty of time for romance when you have your life back together.

Although you may have avoided many of your friends and family members early on in the process of your divorce and recovery, there will come a second stage, when you'll begin to reach out once again. We humans really need contact with others, and this is a time in your life when it's even more important than usual.

One of the most important things to know about making and renewing relationships is that your attitude will be contagious. If you approach others depressed, dragging your tail behind you, and seeking sympathy, you'll find a few rescuers, but not many intimate friends. On the other hand, if you express genuine interest in the other person, her needs, her activities, her interests, you'll increase your chances of success ten times over. We know, and your family members and friends likely know, that you've been going through a rough time lately. And — with some notable exceptions that we discussed earlier in this chapter — most will be sympathetic. But if you really want to develop closeness and trust, you'll have to express closeness and trust.

In chapter 5, we listed a lot of ways to open your life up to new experiences. That's a really healthy thing to do at any point in life, and it's vital now that you're creating a new good life for yourself. And those new activities and experiences and groups are a great place to open yourself up to new relationships — some of which might have the potential for an intimate friendship. Spend some time in a volunteer organization, for instance, and you're almost certain to connect with a few like-minded folks you'll meet later for coffee, or join for dinner, or jog with on Saturday morning. Call a cousin you've only exchanged holiday cards with for ten years, and get reacquainted. When you get past the "how're you doing" superficialities, you're likely to discover someone whose heart is in the right place. She'll have your best interests at heart, even if she's a thousand miles away.

And speaking of long-distance relationships, keep in mind that, while cell phones, email, and text messaging are marvelous new ways to cultivate relationships, you don't want to use them to avoid reaching out to folks closer to home. Virtual hugs are great, but a real shoulder to cry on, or a smiling face to share your little joys with, can't be beat!

Create a strong support system for yourself by cultivating old and new friendships. Rediscover the joys of supportive family ties. Give yourself the gift of closeness, and share it with others. Make at least one "life-line" friend — someone you're willing to take calls from at 3:00 A.M., and who's willing to do the same for you. You'll live longer and be happier — and so will those you share yourself with!

AfterWords — Chapter Eleven

Key Points in the Chapter

- Parents may well object to your divorce, regardless of how supportive they are of you.

- Some family members or friends will pester you for details, offer bad advice, tell you how wrong you are, or tell you things you don't want to know about your ex. If you can't ignore these folks, tell them firmly to change the subject.

- You may find it hard to maintain a close relationship with married friends.

- Some "friends" may shy away now that you're divorced, for a variety of reasons. Be sure you're not sending them away by talking constantly about yourself and your divorce.

- Work at making new friends, but don't give up on your old ones. Especially in the early stages of your divorce process, friends and family are much more important to you than romance.

Activity of the Week

- In your journal, make a list of your close family members and friends. Beside each name, put an "A" or "B" or "C" to note whether the person is (A) someone you trust and can talk with easily about personal things, or (B) someone you see a lot, but aren't sure you feel comfortable telling your life story, or (C) someone with whom you're pretty sure you don't want to discuss the divorce. Create an action plan for increasing the time you spend with your A-list.

Suggested Readings and Resources

Alberti, R.E. and Emmons, M.L. (2001). *Your Perfect Right: Assertiveness and Equality in Your Life and Relationships* (eighth edition). Atascadero, CA: Impact Publishers.

Bloomfield, H. (1996). *Making Peace With Your Parents.* New York: Random House.

Goodman, E. and O'Brien, P. (2001). *I Know Just What You Mean: The Power of Friendship in Women's Lives.* New York: Simon & Schuster.

Sheehy, S. (2000). *Connecting: The Enduring Power of Female Friendship.* New York: W.W. Norton.

Temlock, M. (2006). *Mom, Dad...I'm Getting a Divorce.* Atascadero, CA: Impact Publishers.

12
....

Dealing with Your Ex

THE MARRIAGE IS OVER, and whether you're sad or glad about it, chances are you'd be perfectly happy not to see him again. If *you* ended the marriage, it's only natural if you'd prefer not to have anything more to do with him. (Though certainly there are some women who say, "As a husband he was a washout, but as a friend he's great.") If *he* ended the marriage against your wishes, running into him again might be a bittersweet experience that's more bitter than sweet.

Yes, there are plenty of cases in which former spouses remain on good terms with each other. Cynthia knows a woman on such good terms with her first ex-husband that, even though she's now married to her third husband, Ex Number One remains a good friend (and still does handyman work for her when she needs him). Dr. Bob's divorced parents — both remarried — remained friends until they died. But such stories, though heartwarming, are the exception, not the rule.

"See Ya 'Round"

The rule, however, includes the fact that, whether you want to see him again or not, unless one of you has moved from the area, your paths almost surely will cross. Naturally this is most true if you have kids together. If they're young, he'll most likely be coming to your house to pick them up and drop them off on some sort of regular basis. Even if they're old enough to make it to Dad's house on their own (driving, walking, or taking the bus), or perhaps grown and gone, you're still going to run into him. There will be graduations, weddings, baptisms, brises, christenings, bar and bas mitzvahs, birthday parties, funerals, and other family functions.

And even if you have no kids, if you both still live in the same community, you're still going to meet up someday, somehow. You may both be invited to the same cocktail party, both attend the same charity gala or other event, or even cross paths in such mundane venues as the supermarket, the bank, or the dentist's office. If you're both in the same career field, you may even run into him in the course of business.

What are the hazards of running into him, how do you handle them, and what are the reasons for trying to maintain a civil — if not friendly — relationship with him? That's what this chapter is about.

When It's a Set-Up

In an extreme example, friends who have an "agenda" may even contrive to have you and your ex run into each other unexpectedly (unexpectedly for the two of you — not for the friend who set it up!) at the home of the friend or at some other location. Again, they may have any of a number of different reasons for doing this.

> Donna was devastated when Eric asked for a divorce. She still loved him, but he made it clear that he didn't love her anymore. Several of her friends became aware, after the fact, that there was another woman in Eric's life. Two of them even tried to tell Donna, ever so gently, that this was the case. Donna, still awash in tears, refused to believe it. It was months since the divorce had become final, but she was not yet over her grief.
>
> Her friend Louise decided that Donna would start to heal only after she'd confronted Brittanie, Eric's new lady friend. She learned that Brittanie was an astronomy buff and deduced that Eric and his amour would attend the opening of the new exhibit at the planetarium. Saying nothing of this to Donna, however, Louise pretended interest in the exhibit, said she didn't want to go alone, and asked Donna to accompany her. "It'll do you good to get out of the house," Louise said. When Donna resisted, Louise begged, "Do it for me." Donna reluctantly agreed.
>
> Just as Louise had planned, they saw a lot more than stars and planets at the exhibit; they saw Eric with his new main squeeze, looking very involved with each other.
>
> Donna became so distraught that she and Louise had to leave, and in the weeks that followed, instead of accepting reality as Louise had hoped, she remained devastated, frequently breaking into tears.

Eventually Louise realized she had really messed things up with her maneuver, but that realization didn't help poor Donna.

If Donna is having that much difficulty coming to terms with Eric's departure, she probably could use some short-term counseling, although that's not the point we're trying to make here. Our point is that Louise meddled, thinking she knew what was best for Donna, and she made things worse, not better. Donna, of course, had no way to ward off Louise's machinations; she was blindsided. But if you know or suspect that a friend is trying to engineer you into a situation in which you'll run into your former husband, politely remove yourself from the situation. If need be, distance yourself from the friend.

If It Happens, Deal With It

On the other hand, of course, there are times when you know in advance that you and he are going to be at the same place at the same time. Perhaps some friends are having a big party and don't want to slight either one of you by not inviting you. "Of course we had to invite Tim," they tell you, "but we hope that won't stop you from coming."

And it shouldn't. You don't have to be super-friendly and engage him in conversation if you're not comfortable doing so (though there's no reason you shouldn't if you really want to!), but you can be cordial. No nasty digs. No spilling a drink on him accidentally-on-purpose. No looks that could kill. No barbed comments. Keep it civil. Keep it pleasant. And, if you're not comfortable conversing with him, keep it brief. If it's a large party, there will be plenty of other people there to talk to. You're free to keep your distance.

The same holds true if you run into each other in public. If you find yourself standing in line behind your ex at the bank or at the drugstore checkout, "How've you been?" and "Kind of warm lately, isn't it?" will get you past the awkward moments. It may also help you to realize that he's probably just as flummoxed as you are.

How Friendly Should You Get with Him?

There are some ex-husbands who want to stay friendly...*too* friendly. Amorous, in fact. He may drop over to get you to sign your final joint tax form, or to give you a piece of mail he got that belongs to you, or to pick up the hammer he left behind, or to borrow that old suitcase, and while there, he begins to "make suggestions." The approach may be physical: a kiss or a snuggle. The approach may be something along the lines of, "Do you get lonely at night?" We've even heard of one ex who dispassionately proposed an "arrangement" strictly on a "let's-help-each-other-out" basis — kind of a "You scratch my itch and I'll scratch yours" — no emotions involved.

How can you make love with the man you used to be married to and *not* let your emotions get involved?

And, of course, there are some women who are ready to give in. Out of loneliness, sexual neediness, or perhaps thinking this is a way to get him back.

The advice from here? *Don't.*

The intimate relationship between you is over, and it's important for you to get on with your life. The good life in your future does not include a new romance with him. Romantic interludes, however casual, serve only to drag out the process. Letting go — *disentanglement* — is the name of the game now.

And if he persists, don't let him catch you alone again. If you know he's coming over, make sure to have a "chaperone" — a friend or neighbor — on hand. If he rings the bell unexpectedly, tell him "I'm sorry. This isn't a good time. Come back some other time, and please call first!" *And refuse to open the door.* (You have every right to deny him entry to the house unless the court has explicitly given him access. He has no right to come in without your consent. Even if he's there to pick up or drop off the children, you needn't invite him inside.)

"Cordial? Thanks, Don't Mind If I Am!"

On the other hand, if he's not hassling you in any way — sexual advances, belittling comments, or a repeat of behaviors that led to the divorce — it's good if you can keep things pleasant between you. Under these circumstances, there's no reason not to let him visit. You might even feel okay about letting him do repairs around the house, if you're on comfortable terms with each other and neither of you has a hidden agenda.

We're not advocating that you *should* lean on him for help, but we *are* saying that it's okay to do so if there are no snake pits in the relationship. If you're trying to get him back (be honest with yourself!) by keeping him around in a domestic-like situation, or if he's trying to get you back (or trying to get amorous with you), go hire a handyman out of the Yellow Pages or from a business card tacked up at the hardware store. But if you and your ex are on decent terms with no ulterior motives on either side, and you need his help, there's no harm in asking for it.

Traditionally, when an ex-wife leans on her ex-husband it's been most often for handyman help. In today's world, where more women comfortably wield hammers and where men are not as often looked down on if they aren't handy with tools, the help may well be of some other nature. Perhaps even when you were married you called someone in to clean out the gutters, paint the house, or repair the running toilet. But maybe your husband always took care of the car, and now you need help with car maintenance — or negotiating for a new one. Maybe your husband was good with an upholstery needle, repairing the tears in the couch. Maybe he came from a farm family and you didn't, and so he was the one who canned or jarred the fruits or veggies from your garden — or planted and tended to the garden.

If you're on good terms with him and *if* you are sure your motives are beyond reproach — you want only to get the sofa fixed, or the tomatoes put up, or the car repaired — and *if* you are sure *he* has no hidden agenda (and won't mistake your request for help for an "I miss you, I surrender"), then there's no reason not to ask him for help.

Suggestion: If he's an accountant or an attorney or a therapist, don't ask for his help with your taxes or your contracts or your emotional problems. Those are too personal, and potentially complicated with custody, professional ethics, or other issues in the future. Find solid professionals on your own, with recommendations from friends, family, clergy, and other trusted sources.

When It's Pay(back) Day

Since reciprocity is a virtue, and it would be nice to repay his kindness, you can offer something (other than your affections) in return for his help. Food is a traditional payback, though certainly not the only one. The food you offer him need not be in the form of a meal at your house. If you *want* to feed him a dinner at your table, again, you certainly can *if there's no reason not to* — and we've already spelled out the list of reasons not to. If you're just not up for having dinner with him, though, you can cook a main course and freeze it, then offer him the frozen home-cooked goodie and say, "Here — I made this for you. Take it home, put it in your freezer, and nuke it for your main course one night. One good turn deserves another."

Of course, the "good turn" doesn't have to involve cooking. Maybe your forte is gardening, and you'd like to offer to put in some petunias for him. If he'll provide the petunias, you'll provide the labor. Maybe he needs help with writing a brochure for his small business, and writing is right up your alley. Would you feel okay about giving his house a quick cleaning to help him get ready for an upcoming party? How about covering a volunteer parent shift for him at your youngest's elementary classroom so he can have a long weekend?

Here's another yellow flag: Even if you're better at bookkeeping than he is, however, we wouldn't recommend offering to help him reconcile his bank account. He'd probably prefer to keep his finances more private now that you're apart. And just how would *you* feel when you see the checks he wrote to the florist, the jeweler, and the luxury resort, all in the interest of his new girlfriend?

The Other Woman

Speaking of his new girlfriend, that brings us to another scenario: running into, or even socializing with, your ex once he's remarried. If you and he continue to live in the same community, the odds are fairly good that you'll cross paths eventually. Now, of course you *know* that Doug recently remarried; your friends made sure you heard the news. Maybe there was even a write-up in the paper. But you'd never actually *met* Kimberly till now. (Or maybe she's actually someone you knew all along, but you'd never seen her and Doug together.)

Then you went to the Memorial Day parade to watch your daughter march in the band, and Doug was there too...and brought Kimberly. Or you went to the Snyders' engagement party for their daughter, and you were invited and so was Doug...and he brought

Kimberly. Or you went to the garden center one Saturday, seeking perennials for the border by the back fence, and there were Doug and Kimberly shopping for house plants. (Decorating their new abode together. How cozy!)

What do you do?

If your discomfort level is minimal, acknowledge them, be prepared to make polite conversation (remember *they* may be discomfited even if you're feeling reasonably fine about the encounter), but don't draw the meeting out unless they insist. You may want to be prepared for such invitations as these: "Join us over here. You'll be able to see Megan much better when she marches by," or "Isn't this party a bore? Let's find someplace quiet where we can sit. I'd love you and Kimberly to get to know each other better," or "Taylor, would you mind giving us a suggestion for what we should be buying? You always were the plant expert, and I'm afraid Kimberly's thumb is as brown as mine."

If they seem sincere, and *if you're not uncomfortable,* stand at the parade with them, chat with them, give them advice.

But if either you or one of them is uncomfortable, you can cut it short with a plausible excuse: "I told some friends I'd look for them. Sorry, but thanks." "I haven't made the rounds of the party yet. Maybe I'll catch up with you later." Or cut it short with a very straightforward, "I'm not sure I'm sophisticated enough that I'm ready to give my ex-husband suggestions for decorating the house he lives in with his new wife." If you want, you can lighten the tone with, "It sounds like a Noel Coward comedy. But I think I'm miscast for that play."

Obviously running into him with his new wife (or even girlfriend) will be more painful if you're still hurting over the divorce. But even if you were the one who wanted out of the marriage in the first place, don't be taken by surprise if you experience unexpected pangs at seeing him with another woman. It's a very human reaction, and no, it doesn't mean you've made a mistake or you're having second thoughts. Those pangs can stem from an emotion as petty as resenting him for finding happiness, or simply result from the strangeness of seeing the man who was your husband now obviously attached to another woman. There can even be a bit of competitiveness at work here: He's found happiness with someone else before you did. If you were with a man — even a casual date

— when you ran into Doug and Kimberly, the level of discomfort would have gone way down.

So, what should you do when the occasion arises? Nothing, if you're not uncomfortable. But ease yourself out of the situation if you *are* disturbed. And realize that it's perfectly normal to feel this way, even if you're not still mourning the marriage. Don't berate yourself for being human.

Parenting — the Unbreakable Link

Now let's look at the question of dealing with your ex specifically when there are not-yet-grown kids involved, either living with you or with him. In such cases, you almost can't avoid dealing with the man.

We say "almost" because there are always a few cases of the exes going to great lengths to avoid each other, to the extent that the child is picked up from in front of the door, or from a go-between, rather than the ex entering the house. Occasionally this is due to the court imposing a restraining order. It could also occur because one ex or the other simply refuses to face his or her former spouse. If you have obtained a restraining order against your ex — or he has one against you — you're going to have to make special arrangements to transfer the children on visiting days — perhaps via a neutral third party. But if the avoidance is of your own choice, we urge you to rethink it.

Is he *that* obnoxious or abusive even now? Rather than bar him from the house, consider having another person present as a buffer, a friend or neighbor or relative, and not necessarily the same person every time. Don't invite him in. Have the kids ready when he comes for them, and when he returns them, usher them in, say "Goodbye" firmly, and close the door.

Or is it merely that his visits are too awkward or too painful? If that's the case, time — and some divorce process work from chapter 2 — will help heal the jagged wounds. But we urge you to be pleasant to him for the sake of the kids. This does *not* mean you have to invite him in for dinner, or even for a prolonged chat, but don't be curt and rude if he's done nothing to deserve this treatment. Let the kids see that Mom and Dad can still speak civilly and pleasantly to each other, even though they no longer love each other. It will help make the divorce easier on the kids. And you two do both want what's best for the kids, right?

"Would You Like to Stay for Dinner?"

What if you *want* to invite him to have dinner with you? Should you? Suppose that, while he was out with the kids you made a big lasagna, or roasted a huge chicken. You know there's enough for him and aren't uncomfortable at the thought of him joining you for dinner. Should you ask him?

Well, the first thing you have to ask yourself is: What's your motive? (Why did you make that big lasagna, anyway?) Are you trying to get him back? Trying to "normalize" things between you for the sake of the kids? Trying to find a time when you and he can talk about the kids and discuss various matters that are necessary to work out? Assuming your motives pass inspection, the next thing you have to ask yourself is: How is it going to affect the kids to have Dad over for dinner? And that's definitely a two-sided coin. There are a couple of reactions they're likely to have, both good and not-so-good:

❖ They're going to enjoy seeing Dad at the table with them again. And they're going to feel a sense of peace and relaxation to know that Mom and Dad can talk and communicate and relate to each other without fighting (or ignoring each other, or sniping at each other, or whatever your past behaviors were to each other pre-divorce, when things were deteriorating).

❖ But...being human, they're going to hope that maybe this is Step One on the road to a reconciliation. (And we all know that "Hope springs eternal in the human breast.") Maybe Mom and Dad are going to make up? Maybe Dad is going to move back in! Maybe things will be like they used to be, only better, without the fighting (or silences, or sarcasm)!!

❖ There may be a third reaction, too. The kids may be apprehensive for some other reason. For example, in the period before the divorce, were you and your husband so unhappy that your anger sloshed over onto the kids? If so, the kids may now be concerned that having Dad at the table will mean a return to the times when he or you or both of you found fault with every little thing the kids did, or lost your temper at them, or grew angry out of proportion to a minor offense. Or perhaps your ex *always* had a bad temper. Maybe he *always* was unjustly angry at the kids or blew up over trivial offenses. If that's the case, the kids may not look forward to visiting days and may be sorry to see Dad's visit extended beyond the usual cut-off hour.

So what should you do if you think about asking him to stay for some of your meatloaf or lasagna or roast chicken, but realize it will impact on the kids in both a good way and a bad one? Well, consider the *third* possibility: Is there any *other* negative impact likely to ensue besides that of raising false hopes for a reconciliation? If he's the sort who constantly belittles the kids, or has a bad temper, you'd be wise to minimize the time he spends with them. He's entitled to his fair visiting time with the kids, as spelled out in the divorce document or otherwise decreed by the court, but why prolong their potential unhappiness? Don't invite him for dinner. If you want to discuss the kids' plans for the summer, or the possibility of his attending Betsy's third-grade play, or your hopes that he'll volunteer to chaperone Ryan's scout trip, call him on the phone to discuss it.

But if your only concern is that the kids will misread the signals and hope for a reconciliation, the potential good may outweigh the bad. In time they'll see that there is no reunification or "happily ever after" in the cards. But they'll be let down easily, because Mom and Dad will both still be very much in their lives, and able to talk pleasantly to each other as well. By the time the kids recognize and accept that Mom and Dad are *not* going to get back together, they will have also come to see that it's not so bad the way things are. Dad and Mom are still decent to each other. Dad and Mom are both still involved in the kids' lives. And if the occasional dinner together as a "family" doesn't signal that the parents are going to re-cement, well, at least the family is still capable of occasionally acting as a family. And that's better than the way things are for 90 percent of the kids' divorced friends and *their* families. So, all in all, things are pretty all right, given the circumstances.

The same principles hold true, of course, if the shoe is on the other foot: if it's your ex who's got residential custody, and you are returning the kids after a visit and he invites you to stay for dinner.

Of course, if it's not the kids as much as your ex who is reading the signals wrong, that's a whole other kettle of fish. Then you may want to temper your enthusiasm for showing the kids that Mom and Dad can still be friends.

And if it's *you* who wants the reconciliation, remember that marriages that didn't work the first time rarely work on a second go-round. You'd be better advised to spend your time working on getting over him than plotting to get him back.

Be Yourself — Assertively

In the course of the breakup and divorce, you've probably had to deal with pushy attorneys, rigid court systems, uncaring landlords, aggressive bill collectors, and assorted other cold characters who have tested your mettle almost continually. And then there's your ex!

How do you handle these folks and keep your sanity? We're not going to say it's easy, but there are some tips we can offer, starting with this one: *You're never wrong to be yourself.*

The most basic concept we want you to recognize about human relationships is that *we're all equal as human beings.* Nobody, regardless of rank or position or power, is a better *person* than you are. Sure, they may have authority over things that are important to you and/ or your kids, but on a level of human being to human being, you're every bit as valuable, important, and worthy as anyone you'll come across in life. And that absolutely includes your ex.

"So what?" you're asking. "If he holds the most important thing in my life in his hands because he co-parents the kids, or he still controls my main source of financial support, or his name is there with mine on the mortgage, how can I do anything but go along with whatever he wants?"

Legitimate concerns, but the wrong question. The issue is one of *respect*. You've spent a lot of time with this guy over the last few years, and the two of you have developed habits about how you deal with each other. If you typically "went along" in your marriage, it will be hard to change that pattern now. But change it you must. He may not have respected your ideas and opinions before, but it's your job to make damn sure he does now.

Start by behaving as a person *deserving* respect. Take an assertiveness training class (or at least read Dr. Bob's book, *Your Perfect Right*). Learn to state your ideas directly, without hedging or apologizing for what you think. Tell him when he's not listening to you. Memorize the divorce settlement and bring up the court's instructions when you need to. (Be sure you're keeping up your end as well.) Let him know that the old patterns are no good any more, that you expect to be respected, just as he would a co-worker, boss, neighbor, professor or attorney.

We're not advocating that you become "the pushy one" with your ex. We're suggesting that you treat each other as *equals*. You can make that happen if you stand up straight, look him in the eye, state your position without apology, and let him know you expect to negotiate as equals — just as it says in the divorce decree. All this can be done with a smile (unless you're angry) and in a friendly and matter-of-fact way. You needn't be confrontational, unless the situation calls for that because he's not cooperating.

The bottom line here is that — whether the issue is the support check, child management (discipline, bedtime, vacations, visitation, relocating), selling the house, or anything else — neither of you is "in charge." You must work it out together.

Set Clear Limits

Now you know something about being assertive, making sure your point of view is heard, and standing up for yourself. One important extension of that concept is to *set clear limits* with your ex. Some of these points have come up before, but we think they bear repeating — and making clear to him:

Is he welcome in your home? Any limits on hours?

Will you socialize together? Date? Romance? Sex? (Rarely a good idea!)

Who makes decisions about child rearing (school, discipline, health care, etc.): You? He? Both together? Are you flexible about visitation hours and days?

How will money (for example, spousal and child support, proceeds from property, etc.) be handled between you?

Will he help maintain the former family home where you now live with the kids?

Many such details will have been worked out in the divorce itself, and may be mandated by the court (such as rules regarding the children, property). Other items — and the things we've listed here are but a small sampling of examples — are "up for grabs," and how you come out in the grabs will depend on your own assertiveness. To protect your interests, it's really important to be clear — with yourself and with him — just what you want regarding each issue. Communicate it in conversation, write it down and give him a copy, and repeat it when necessary. You needn't offer lengthy explanations for your positions, but you'll be way ahead if your expectations are reasonable.

Don't Badmouth Him to the Kids

One of the toughest issues in divorce recovery when kids are involved is how each parent discusses the ex-partner with the children.

Some unforgiving ex-marrieds want their children to dislike the other parent as much as they do. They go to great lengths to let the kids know what an SOB he was or bitch she was. They forbid the kids to talk about him or her in their presence. They keep visitations to the absolute minimum required by the court and are inflexible about special occasions. The extreme of this approach is a controversial pattern some call "parental alienation syndrome," which involves an active concerted effort by one parent to teach the children to hate the other parent. This idea has strong political overtones related to parental rights and domestic abuse. It's easy to see why it's controversial. Suffice to say that efforts to turn the children against your ex may backfire and are in no one's best interest. If your ex is a monster, you will likely have obtained a court order restraining his contact with the family. If he's not, the children will need to discover for themselves what kind of person he is, and work out their own relationship with him. After all, you loved him once, didn't you?

Jann Blackstone-Ford and Sharyl Jupe, in their book *Ex-Etiquette for Parents*, point out that, "If you say something negative about your former spouse to your child, it hurts the child, not your ex."

Don't Make Kids the Messenger

We've said it before, but here it comes again: When the two of you have matters to work out — whether the simplest scheduling questions or the most difficult conflicts over money or custody — figure out a way to communicate directly. *Don't ask your kids to carry messages* back and forth between you. Kids have a hard enough time dealing with the day-to-day stresses of living in two homes, dividing their loyalties, and growing up. It's not fair to expect them to be your channel of communication. ("While you're there, tell your father that the support check is late, and you need clothes for school.") Use email, the phone, letters, faxes, whatever works for you — but *not* the kids.

Put Together a "Parenting Plan" — In Writing

A more-or-less "formal" parenting agreement is a powerful tool in heading off conflict between you and your ex. You may think it unnecessary to create a detailed document, but you'll be glad you did when trouble rears its ugly noggin.

Getting it in writing from the get-go may save you a ton of headache and heartache down the road. Here are some of the elements of a thorough agreement between ex-spouses:

❖ *General Philosophy.* This part is just a "preamble" that essentially says you want to work out your differences cooperatively and responsibly, putting the needs of the children first. A summary of the court-ordered custody rules can go here too.

❖ *Parenting Schedule.* Here's where you spell out where the kids will be when. School schedules, visitation, vacation, holidays, activities, birthdays … the more detailed this plan, the fewer sources of arguments about it later.

❖ *Parental Contributions.* Somebody has to pay for the kids' living expenses. The court will have ordered if there is to be child support, and dictated the general terms and amounts of payment. Still, you'll inevitably run into situations that require negotiation. Put the ground rules for those negotiations down in advance, before the incidents come up. Who pays for gym shoes, special sports equipment, tuba lessons, soccer camp, prom dresses, dental care, car insurance when they start to drive, uniforms, and so on?

❖ *Communication and Conflict Resolution.* This is complicated — the subject of many books. Still, you can lay out some ground rules in your parenting agreement, and they may help you over the rough spots later. What will you put in writing to be sure both ex-partners have the same information? Who decides "the best interests of the children?" Will you call on a mediator when you simply can't agree?

❖ *Miscellaneous.* Here's where you cover all the other stuff you can think of that might come up. How to deal with illnesses, out-of-town travel, phone and email contact, transportation, bedtime rules, homework rules, curfews, emergency notification, relocation.

The ideas here come mostly from Dr. Phil Stahl's excellent book, *Parenting After Divorce,* and are based on the work of Robert LaCrosse, Ph.D., a psychologist in Denver, Colorado, and William Hilton, an attorney in San Jose, California, who originally developed aspects of the Sample Parenting Agreement that appears in Dr. Stahl's book.

Incidentally, if dealing with your ex has become impossible, there are special professionals appointed by the court who may be available in your community to help protect the best interests of your children. Called "parenting coordinators," these psychologists, social workers, or other mental health professionals are skilled in evaluation, mediation, education, and counseling, and it's their job to make sure the children's interests are put first. If you're having a particularly difficult time working out a parenting plan with your ex, make a call to the clerk of the family court and inquire about the availability of a parenting coordinator.

Winning the Battle of the Exes

Despite the final decree you have tucked away in your desk, your ex is likely to be in your life at some level for a long time, especially if you have children together. You're going to waste too much of your life energy on him if you don't let yourself get over it. It will take time, and a considerable effort, but you *can* get over it. You might want to go back over this chapter from time to time as you work your way through the feelings and issues.

A couple of final thoughts:

❖ *You can't change him.* You couldn't while you were married, and you have even less influence now. Don't waste your energy.

❖ *You can change the way you see him.* He's not the enemy. He's a shadow in your past, and your job from now on is to shine a light on the good life in your future.

AfterWords — Chapter Twelve

Key Points in the Chapter

- You and your ex are very likely to run into each other from time to time, even if you don't have children. You need to be prepared to deal with that.

- It may be tempting to maintain or re-establish an intimate relationship with your ex. Don't.

- As best you can, remain cordial friends with your ex, particularly for the sake of the children.

- You'll probably feel some discomfort when/if you see him with another woman. Admit that will happen, and learn to accept and get past it.

- Be assertive in your relationship with him. You deserve respect — both from him and from yourself.

- If you haven't already done so, work out a detailed written parenting plan, and stick to it.

Activity of the Week

- Which of the following patterns describes your relationship with your ex? (More than one may apply.)

  He's dominant. You're helpless.

  He'll agree to anything you want.

  He threatens you and the children.

  You don't talk to one another.

  You are cordial friends.

  You communicate only as much as necessary for parenting and financial matters.

- Are you satisfied with your current relationship?

- Write down action steps you can take to improve the situation. (For example, talk it over with him, become more assertive with him, learn to relax, propose revisions to your parenting plan, talk to your therapist, talk to your attorney.)

Suggested Readings and Resources

Alberti, R.E. and Emmons, M.L. (2001). *Your Perfect Right: Assertiveness and Equality in Your Life and Relationships* (eighth edition). Atascadero, CA: Impact Publishers.

Blackstone-Ford, J. & Jupe, S. (2004). *Ex-Etiquette for Parents: Good Behavior After a Divorce or Separation*. Chicago: Chicago Review Press.

Margulies, S. (2004). *A Man's Guide to a Civilized Divorce*. Emmaus, PA: Rodale Press.

Phelps, S. & Austin, N. (2002). *The Assertive Woman* (fourth edition). Atascadero, CA: Impact Publishers.

Wenning, K. (1998). *Men Are from Earth, Women Are from Earth*. New York: Jason Aronson.

13

• • • • • • • • • •

Dating Again

OONER OR LATER, YOU'RE LIKELY to think in terms of dating again.
When is the right time?

There is no hard-and-fast timetable, of course, but you'll find it helpful to wait till you're over most of whatever bitterness or mistrust you feel as a result of your recent divorce. We're not saying you have to be completely free of all negative emotions — that's asking too much of yourself. But at least wait till the strongest emotions — fear, grief, anger — have subsided. Otherwise, your mistrust or animosity is likely to carry over toward the men you date.

And date when *you're* ready. Not when your friends start telling you, "It's time to get out and meet some guys." Not just because your cousin's husband has a friend your cousin thinks would be perfect for you, and "good catches don't wait around forever." Not because your best friend says, "Do you want people to think you're bitter?" or "Do you want to be alone for the rest of your life?"

When the prospect of spending an evening with a new man is more intriguing than upsetting (even if it feels a bit daunting), when an evening out with your friends no longer satisfies your need to get out, when you feel you're ready for a bit of an adventure, or when you specifically crave male companionship — and not just that of Joe-who's-like-a-brother-to-you or the guys from work who are your buddies — then it's time to think about dating.

What's So Great About Dating, Anyway?

Your divorce wounds may still be raw, and you're in no way ready to venture back out into the dating world. Fair enough. Chances are, however, that eventually you will...even if you're not thinking about marriage. Many divorced women who have no intention of marrying again still date, for an assortment of reasons, including:

❖ Companionship

❖ Interesting and stimulating conversation on a variety of topics

❖ A male partner for couple-oriented functions, such as dinner parties and social events

❖ A male partner for casual dinners, movies, theater, games, and other such events

❖ The excitement of attraction, flirtation, and romance, even though no permanent commitment is desired

❖ Sexual gratification

Ready for a Trip to the "Meet" Market?

When you do start thinking about dating, you may be wondering, "Where does a divorcée go to meet men?" That part has changed some, but for the most part, you'll find eligible men in the same places you met men as a first-time-around single:

❖ Through your work — guys who work with you, clients, suppliers, consultants, customers, colleagues in your profession, and others you meet in the course of business. (Be careful about company policies and water-cooler gossip!);

❖ Through an introduction from a friend, relative, neighbor, or other contact;

❖ At any club or organization you belong to (don't just join — take part);

❖ At any class you might be taking (class discussion, breaks, after-class coffee...);

❖ Through your kids (they may have friends with divorced dads);

❖ At a dance or other social event, especially one promoted for singles;

❖ At a bar or other establishment heavily frequented by singles (yeah, well…);

❖ At the library or a bookstore (if you're looking at the same shelf, there's an opener);

❖ At a concert (go for refreshments at intermission!);

❖ At a museum or gallery (art makes great conversation);

❖ In the course of your everyday life: The mailman, the new neighbor, the butcher in the supermarket, or your son's geometry teacher may be single, interested, and interesting;

❖ And don't overlook the Personals section of your local newspaper and its on-line counterpart, E-dating services.

Of course, there's no guarantee that the "Handsome, divorced, thoughtful forty-five-year-old" advertised in the paper or online isn't really funny-looking, still married, self-centered, or seventy…or all of the above! But liars and cheaters aren't found only amid the columns of newsprint or the electrons on your computer screen. Married men have been attending singles dances, or pocketing their wedding rings before frequenting singles bars, since half-past forever. In person, they can't lie about their looks, but they can and often do lie about much else, including their marital status.

So should you avoid answering ads in the Personals or joining an on-line matchmaking service? Not necessarily. Proceed with caution, be very slow to give out your home phone number, and be sure to meet the guy in a public place the first time or two — ideally with a friend in tow. Observe all sensible precautions. Not only could the guy be a liar, he could actually be dangerous…but then, so could someone you meet in the library or at church. The newspapers are full of stories in which the neighbors are quoted as saying, "It's so hard to believe the police have the right man. He was always so nice to us, he seemed so good to his family, and he went to church every Sunday morning." There are no guarantees in this world. You need to be cautious, to be vigilant, and to listen to your own instincts.

What Will It Be Like This Time Around?

How is dating different for a divorcée than for a never-been-married single person?

❖ You are probably carrying some residual emotional baggage: mistrust, or resentment as a result of your last bad experience.

❖ Your virginity is not an issue, though whether and when to be physically intimate is still very much a question.

❖ If you've been married since 1980 or earlier, you've never before dated in the age of AIDS. The last time you were dating, unprotected sex could lead to a pregnancy or a curable STD, but not to a so-far-incurable and ultimately fatal disease.

❖ You may have children now, which will impact on your dating. There are multiple issues here: you want to date men who will eventually accept and be good to your kids if this relationship is going anywhere, but you also don't want to bring home every man you ever have one date with. Too, if the kids are home with a babysitter, you'll need to be home by a particular time. (Shades of your teen years, when you had a curfew!) And if you and your gentleman-friend are headed for the bedroom, we suggest you make it *his* bedroom if your kids are at home.

Besides the differences between dating as a divorcée and dating as an unmarried single, there are the differences between dating *now* and dating *then*. If you were married only five years, dating customs probably haven't changed much since your last time around. But if you were married a substantial length of time, you may be unaccustomed to paying for some of your dates or for some part of your dates (for example, he pays for dinner, you pay for the movie). And you may be uncomfortable asking a man out. Yet these things are all done now...not universally, to be sure, but often enough not to be unusual any more.

Getting Physical

Okay, sooner or later we have to get to the subject that's on everybody's mind when we talk about dating: sexual affection between you and your new friend. There are two types of situations in particular that you're likely to face when you start dating seriously, unless you keep your dates exceedingly chaste.

Molly considers herself neither a prude nor a wild thing. She dated Jack for several months before she finally became sexually intimate with him, and then she took care never to make love with him when the children were in the house. They made love only when the kids were at their dad's or at a friend's for the night, or when she and Jack were at his house. (His kids are grown and gone.)

Molly has two girls, eleven-year-old Eileen and fifteen-year-old Amanda. She is fairly strict with Amanda and has raised her to respect her body, hold on to her virginity, and not let boys go "too far" when she's out on dates.

One evening, after both Eileen and Amanda had gone to bed. Jack and Molly were in the living room. Eventually, they wound up on the couch, snuggling, which led to kissing, and the kissing led to Jack's hand making its way to Molly's breast.

They didn't hear Amanda get out of bed and head to the kitchen for a glass of juice. They didn't hear her till she was in the room, staring at them. At that point Amanda called her mother a hypocrite, screeching, "How come it's all right for you but not for me?! Well, I don't respect your rules anymore. I don't respect *you* anymore!" And she stormed out.

Naturally Molly tried to explain to Amanda that the rules for a fifteen-year-old are different from those for a grown woman, that the rules for a virgin are different from those for a woman with Molly's experience, and that Jack has more self-control than the boys Amanda dates. But teenagers aren't noted for being reasonable and sensible, and Amanda isn't the first teenager to rage at what she views as a double standard.

Is there a best way to handle this situation? Molly's efforts to explain seem reasonable enough, but there are too many variables for us to offer a general rule. How old your kids are, what values you've tried to instill in them, how physically progressed your own relationship is. For now, the important thing is to raise the question, so that you're prepared in your own mind should the day that may come when your kids catch you necking — or more — with your gentleman friend one evening. You won't be caught short — stammering and blushing — if you've thought this through in advance and are prepared with an answer.

The concept of "safer sex" enters the picture about here. Amanda — and Molly — need to be up to date on the issues surrounding sexually transmitted diseases, HIV, AIDS, and the current technology of protection. We offer for your consideration the *Impact Publishers Statement on Safe Sex* (see Appendix I) as a set of standards for evaluating the risks.

Which brings us to the next situation and question: When, if ever, should you let your gentleman friend spend the night at your house while the kids are there?

Again, it's not our place to lecture you on morality; indeed, we don't mean to frame our answer in terms of morality. There are some perfectly wonderful mothers who have long-term live-in relationships with men, men who are their "husbands" in all but legality. And there are also mothers who would never be physically intimate with a man until marriage. In addition, there are women who make a variety of choices in between.

If it isn't our place — or even our wish — to make moral value judgments for you, what is there for us to say on the subect? Simply this: If you do choose to have "sleepovers" with your gentleman friend, do it wisely. Remember that you are modelling for your kids. If you have one serious boyfriend, and you allow him to spend the night sometimes, that's one thing. If you have plural boyfriends spending the night, however, or if you are "serially monogamous" — seeing and making love with only one man at a time in your life, but changing boyfriends every few months — you are modelling as acceptable a pattern of behavior that you may find very unacceptable when your kids begin to imitate your lifestyle.

Of course, there are differences between your living this way and your sixteen-year-old daughter doing the same, but try explaining that to her! (And even if she's only nine or ten now, don't think she won't remember when she's sixteen — she will.)

So, should you *ever* let a gentleman friend spend the night? That's something you have to decide for yourself. Should you let an *assortment* of gentlemen friends spend the night? Consider the consequences — for your children and for yourself.

"Why Can't I Do That, Mom?"

What about other boundaries that you set for your daughter or son but don't observe yourself? Again, it's not our place to set moral standards for you, but we do urge you to have answers at the ready concerning why it's OK for Molly to let her boyfriend do something (you fill in the blank) even though she tells Amanda and Eileen never to let a boy do the same.

Whether we're talking about actual lovemaking or lesser degrees of intimacy, there are defensible viewpoints. Here are a few examples to get you started on coming up with your own answers, depending upon your own views:

❖ "Men of Jack's age have better will power. They can 'put on the brakes' *much* better than boys your age can."

❖ "At my age, I won't get a bad reputation. You will!"

❖ "Possible pregnancy is not an issue with me."

❖ "I know the risks of sexually transmitted diseases, and how to protect myself against them. And I do what's necessary."

❖ "I'm not a virgin. You are. And I'd like you to stay that way."

❖ "At my age, I know the difference between love and sex. You're smart for your age, but you're still only sixteen."

❖ "If it matters to you what others think of you at school and among your friends, I think you'll agree with me that you should wait till you're older."

❖ "Your first sexual experience should be very special, with someone you really care about. I don't think you're ready for that kind of commitment."

Are You Really Ms. Right?

Whenever you do start dating again, and whether you have kids or not, don't enter the dating arena in panic mode and don't do it with a chip on your shoulder. The woman in panic mode fears that she's going to be alone and jumps at the first opportunity she has for involvement. She will probably marry Mr. Wrong. The woman with a chip on her shoulder is so determined not to make the same mistake again and so convinced that men are stinkers that she will likely turn her back on Mr. Right.

The smart woman will not only take her time before she re-enters the dating arena but will also realize that the first man she meets is in all likelihood not her Galahad, no matter how shining his armor seems. Is it totally impossible that the first man she dates will be perfect for her? Not totally *impossible*, just awfully *unlikely*. What's more probable is that he's so different from her ex that he seems exceedingly right, and she — having been alone for a while now and unhappily married before that — will mistake him for Mr. Right, when he's really Mr. Better (but not good enough).

You Sure Can Pick 'Em!

Now let's look at two other mistakes some people — both women and men — commit. We touched on one of them a minute ago.

Many people are repeatedly attracted to the same type. In some cases, this can lead to making the same mistake over and over. Case in point: the woman who is attracted to men with strong personalities, but always winds up picking someone domineering or bossy, traits she ultimately can't live with.

On the other hand, some people coming out of a bad relationship (marital or otherwise) will deliberately seek out a new romantic partner who is the polar opposite of the person he or she recently divorced. The woman who does this may find a man who is completely different from her ex-husband, and become fixated on the fact that he doesn't display the same traits that bothered her in her marriage. She'll fail to realize that, though he lacks those faults, he has several others that are equally troublesome. Or she'll fail to take note of the fact that, while he doesn't have any of her ex-husband's bad points, this new guy doesn't have any of her ex's good points either!

Your best choice of a new male friend (or eventual new husband) is someone who's truly your *friend*. Some of the best and deepest love relationships are between two people who describe each other as "my best friend."

But whether or not marriage is your ultimate goal, take your time as you begin dating. Don't rush into a new relationship, and if you find one that suits you, don't rush into turning it into a marriage. Consider this insight from Dr. Helen Fisher, anthropologist at Rutgers University, quoted in the *New York Times* in June 2005:

"When you're in the throes of...romantic love it's overwhelming, you're out of control, you're irrational..."

In fact, a good question is whether you should remarry at all. We'll discuss that question in chapter 15.

Are You Ready?

There is no magic about the timing of "when to start dating again." It's a very personal choice and depends upon your own comfort level with the dating process. The most general advice we can offer is "go slowly." Take your time. Think of each new relationship as a learning experience.

Dr. Bruce Fisher, whose "rebuilding" model of divorce recovery we examined in chapter 2, emphasized the importance of working through your divorce process before you begin to seek new *serious* relationships. He was, however, an advocate of "transitional" or "growing" relationships. He encouraged those quasi-romantic relationships that allow you to get to know yourself better, to grow, to move beyond the relationship that has ended, and to develop a better sense of your goals for a future long-term relationship. Bruce was fond of saying, "Relationships are your teachers."

Dating can help you figure out where you are now, so you can decide where you go from here.

When you were younger — maybe very young — you probably dated a number of people before you found the one you then considered "Mr. Right" — even though he eventually turned out to be "Mr. Wrong." That's not a bad way to approach your new life, either. Chances are good that you'll have a few growing relationships before you find a new long-term love. And that's a good thing. Enjoy yourself. Date a variety of people. Experiment a little. If you're open to new experiences, these transitional relationships can be great teachers!

What About the Kids?

We don't have to tell you that your children are a major influence in your love life. Who you date, where, when and how are very much caught up in your role as mom to the rugrats, little-leaguers, and teenagers in your house. As you might guess, we're got something to say on that subject, too.

But you'll have to turn the page....

AfterWords — Chapter Thirteen

Key Points in the Chapter

- Begin dating again only when *you* are ready.

- Look for available men in the same places you met them before your marriage: work, mutual friends, volunteer organizations, the library, bookstores, concerts, ball games, galleries, personal ads.

- Remember that things are different now. Consider: your emotional baggage, your kids, STDs, societal changes in man-woman relationships.

- As you develop new intimate relationships, be prepared to deal with the issue of how your children will handle waking up with a strange man in the house, and how you will set boundaries for your teenagers that you don't observe yourself.

- Be careful not to repeat destructive patterns from your past relationships.

- Keep the dates pretty casual until you have done the work of emotional recovery outlined in chapter two.

Activity of the Week

Time for some serious introspection. Make some notes about where you're headed with dating:

- Take an honest look at yourself this week. Are you the kind of person you'd like to date? Are you pretty well over the ending of your marriage? Are you ready to resist repeating the errors you made last time around? Are you taking care of yourself, emotionally and physically, so that you'd be attractive to the kind of man you'd like to date? Are you someone others find fun to be with? What do you "bring to the table" in a romantic exchange?

- And what about him? Have you given some serious thought to the sort of man you're interested in? Are you looking for someone to have fun with, or a potential husband, or a father figure for your kids, or a stable source of financial support, or what? Does he need to be a "hunk"? How about his intellectual interests? Is politics important? Religion? Personal habits?

Suggested Readings and Resources

Browne, J. (1997). *Dating for Dummies.* New York: For Dummies/ Wiley.

Ellis, A. and Crawford, T. (2000). *Making Intimate Connections: Seven Guidelines for Great Relationships and Better Communication.* Atascadero, CA: Impact Publishers.

Fisher, B. and Hart, N. (2000). *Loving Choices: An Experience in Growing Relationships.* Atascadero, CA: Impact Publishers.

Impact Publishers Statement on Safer Sex (see Appendix I)

Online resources: *www.e-harmony.com* is a popular and well-researched "matchmaking" site.

Search "dating" in your favorite browser and be prepared for thousands of hits!

14

•••••••••

The Other Dating Game: Kids 2, Dates 0

HOW WILL YOU TELL YOUR KIDS that you're starting to date again? And what will their reactions be?

Don't be surprised if a young child asks you, "Are you going to marry this man?" after just one date. Little ones don't have great comprehension of the dating process.

On the other hand, don't be surprised if the kids try to do everything they can think of to interfere. This can include:

❖ Begging you not to go out on a date;

❖ Developing a tummyache or other ailment and begging you not to go out and leave them with a sitter when they don't feel well;

❖ Calling your cellphone every ten minutes while you're out on your date;

❖ Being on their worst behavior if your date comes to the house to pick you up.

Why do kids want to keep their divorced parents from dating?

❖ They feel you're being disloyal to Daddy. (Sit the kids down, explain to them that you're not married to Daddy anymore, nor is Daddy married to you, and so you're both free to date other people.)

❖ They're still hoping you and Daddy will get back together. If your dating leads to marriage, and you marry someone else, you won't be able to marry Daddy again. (Of course, you've already explained to them that there is zero chance of you and their dad getting back together, whether or not you marry someone else, right? You can also point out that just because you're dating someone doesn't mean you're going to marry him.)

❖ They have a friend whose mom remarried, and the new husband isn't good to the kids. They're afraid of a similar outcome. (Assure them that you would not marry anyone who wasn't kind and good and caring to your children.)

❖ They just don't want "a stranger" living in their house. (Explain to them that if and when you do decide to marry someone else, he will have gotten to know the kids so well by that point that he won't be a stranger at all.)

❖ The kids enjoy having all your attention and don't want to share it. (Explain to them that you need the companionship of people your own age — both women and men. Point out that, as much as they love you, your kids wouldn't want to spend all their time with only you. They need friends their own ages too. And so do you.)

It's usually better to meet new men at some location other than your house, at least for the first few dates. This is not only for the obvious safety factor of not exposing your home (and children) to someone you don't know. It's also best if your kids don't see you dating a parade of different men, which could potentially upset them. Moreover, it's best if your kids don't get attached to some man who isn't going to be in your life for very long.

So, if this is your first or second date with Rick, rather than having him pick you up at your house, suggest meeting him at the restaurant, theater, coffee shop, or other destination. When the kids ask, "Who are you going to the movies with? One of your friends?" you can say, "No, with a man." If they ask, "Is it Bob again?" you can certainly answer truthfully, "No, it's someone new." But they don't have to meet him right away.

When you feel that a man is someone you're really interested in getting to know better, someone you hope you'll be seeing for a while, then it might be time for him to meet your kids. While you don't want them getting attached to several different men who ultimately don't stick around in your life — whether through your choice or theirs or his — it is important that anyone you think has serious potential meets the kids. You need to see how he reacts to them, and how they react to him.

Remember, though, that their reactions may very possibly be colored by factors that have nothing to do with his suitability. On the one hand, they may be so resentful of anyone who is not Dad that they'll spurn him, even if he's Mr. Totally Wonderful. Conversely, if they've truly accepted that Dad's gone from their household, and they're hungry to have a father figure in their lives, they might glom onto him voraciously, even if he's Mr. Less-Than-Average.

At some point, if the relationship shows signs of becoming serious, you'll want to begin including the kids in some of your activities with him. This can mean simply having him over for dinner with all of you, or going somewhere together. "Somewhere" can be as simple as the local movie theater, or a ball game, or a nearby park to fly kites, or your favorite pizza haunt. That first all-together-now event probably should not involve any real distance. It could be a *long* trip home if things don't go well!

Before too many dates, however, you'll want to see how the kids react to Mr. New-in-Your-Life, and how Mr. New reacts to the kids, not just for a half hour or the length of a dinner at home, but for a more extended time, and under circumstances when the kids aren't necessarily on their best behavior.

How does Mr. New handle it if little Will throws a temper tantrum or turns whiny? What does he say to Tanya when she's bossy, stubborn, or argumentative, or says, "I don't have to listen to you. You're not my daddy!"

You can learn a lot by observing the way the kids react to Mr. New and, especially, the way Mr. New reacts to the kids.

What Would You Expect Them to Say?

Don't be surprised if the kids are jealous of your new friend's attentions to you, or yours to him. This is true of *any* new male friend — even a first date — not just one who's getting serious with you. With no husband in your household, the kids have been the most important people in your life. Now, suddenly, you're dating, and you're paying serious attention to one or more men.

No wonder the kids might feel put out that someone else commands your attention. This new person is not only taking Dad's place, he is usurping their space as Most Important People in your life. So, don't be surprised if Alison suddenly develops a tummyache when you're getting prepared for a date, or Megan calls you seven times on your cell phone while you're out with a man.

How do you handle this?

With understanding and firmness. If you have reason to suspect that Alison's tummyache is, if not outright invented, at least not physical in origin, and if you know you're leaving her in good hands (Grandma, your sister, or a very reliable, mature babysitter), go ahead and go out. And if the kids keep calling your cell while you're out on a date, tell them that there had better be fire trucks or police cars parked at the house when you get home if they call again. That nothing short of a bona fide emergency warrants one more call from them. Or tell them you want no more calls from them. If there is truly a crisis or major problem, they're to tell the sitter, and if something *really* is wrong, the sitter — and *only* the sitter — may call you.

Of course, their calls may not be a ploy to disrupt your date, or a move born of jealousy. They may simply miss having you at home and have a total lack of understanding or respect for your need for an evening out. If you've been going out evenings with some regularity — with friends, or to classes, or to events such as meetings or concerts or poetry-readings — then the kids are used to your absenting yourself from the house on some evenings. But what if you've been staying home evening after evening with the kids, and only now — when you're finally dating again — are you first beginning to go away from the house and the kids? It's going to be harder for them to get used to your absences, at least for a while.

How Does He Treat the Kids?

What do you do when you like a guy, but you don't like the way he relates to your kids? Do you give up a romance with Mr. Ideal because he's Mr. Not-So-Ideal in the parenting department?

As with so many other issues in life, there's no cut-and-dried answer to this one either. Is he an experienced dad or new at the game? If he's got kids of his own, it's not a matter of lack of experience or knowledge; you just don't like his parenting style. That doesn't necessarily make him *wrong*. But your style of parenting and his differ, and very possibly don't mesh well at all.

(We're assuming here that he's not outright cruel or thoughtless. If he is, that's a different story. Say goodbye and move on.)

It's *possible* you could get him to change his style with time. It's also *unlikely*. On the other hand, many first marriages consist of moms and dads whose parenting styles differ. If your methodologies differ, but you agree on fundamentals — such as the core values you wish to teach the kids — all is not necessarily lost. One of you can be more strict than the other, or one may believe in explaining the reasons for rules while the other believes in "because I say so." One may believe in punishing only with timeouts while the other believes in suspension of privileges or allowance. None of these automatically has to be a "deal-breaker."

And then, it may be that he's simply new at this game, never had kids, has no experience raising them, and just doesn't know what he's doing. Unless he's the sort who thinks he's always right about everything (and if he is, you may want to run, not walk, to the nearest exit, for a lot of reasons that have nothing to do with a clash in parenting styles), you may be able to persuade him that your methods of parenting are effective and worth adopting.

But do study how he relates to your kids. If you strongly disapprove of the way he handles them, and he won't alter his methods, or there's something inherently unkind about the way he acts with them, or if he doesn't respect them and their rights as people, he's your Mr. Wrong, no matter how right he seems when the two of you are alone together. The parenting issues will drive a large wedge between you that will only grow larger with time.

The first obvious difference will be that he'll parent *your* kids in ways you won't approve of — which will agonize you as well as antagonize you. Then, your Mr. Wrong is bound to needle you that it's *your* fault when, inevitably, seven-year-old Abigail misbehaves on a bad day, or teenage Terry shoplifts a sweater or experiments with alcohol at a friend's house, despite their careful and caring upbringing. Had you brought the kids up *his* way, he'll insist, this never would have happened.

Of course that's hogwash. All kids go astray sometimes. But you'll be in a bad position for making that point at the moment.

So watch the way he relates to your kids, talk to him about his parenting methods, and if you and he aren't on the same page, honestly appraise the chances of this relationship working:

❖ Might he change his ways and his thinking?

❖ If not, can you compatibly raise the kids together anyhow?

❖ Or are your differences deal-breakers?

The way your kids relate to him is really important, but check out carefully what's really going on. Remember that their reactions to him might be influenced by those other factors: feeling that you're being disloyal to Dad; being bothered by the knowledge that if you marry this new guy, you'll *never* get back with Dad; and feeling jealous of anyone else who takes your time and attention away from them.

So if the kids are less than enthusiastic about your new guy, remember that their reactions *might* be something less than fair toward him. Yes, they might be seeing something unlovely and unlovable in him that you're too enamored to see clearly. But they also might be viewing the relationship through very jaundiced and very unfair eyes.

How Will He Win Them Over?

Kids often don't accept a new man in Mom's life, at least not right away. And sometimes, in an effort to win the kids over, the new man will try too hard to get them to like him, thereby setting up unrealistic expectations.

This campaign to earn the kids' affections can take a number of forms. The man may buy the kids presents. He may take them on many fun excursions. Or he may simply spend inordinate amounts of time with them at home playing catch, video games, card or board games, or teaching them to cook, to do woodworking, or play chess.

All of these activities, of course, are great when done in moderation. They're what you hope any man *would* do with your kids if he were to become a part of the family. The problem is one of *quantity*. Is he buying them too many presents and spoiling them? Is he setting them up for an expectation that this is what life with him will always be like — frequent presents, an unrealistic number of excursions, or a greater amount of time spent with them than he can possibly maintain on an ongoing basis? In short, is he acting out the "Disneyland Dad" role?

In trying to win them over now, he's setting them up to resent him later when he doesn't follow through and keep up the pace.

If It Doesn't Work Out

Sometimes the scenario goes differently. You meet a new man, it seems to be going well between you, so you introduce him to the kids. They all really get along, and everything's going swimmingly with them. Then the relationship hits a snag. Not the relationship between him and the kids, but the relationship between him and you.

You decide (or he does) that things are not going to work out after all. In the meanwhile, the kids have become attached to him. What to do?

Of course, avoiding this sort of situation is one very good reason for not introducing your kids to the fellows you date till the relationship really seems to be showing promise. But sometimes you take all the right precautions and things still go awry. What will you do about it? And what will you tell the kids?

Let's take the second question first. There's no one blanket answer. (Have we said that before?) The best answer will depend on a variety of factors:

❖ How old your kids are;

❖ How attached they've become to the guy;

❖ How attached he's become to them;

❖ How sure you are that the relationship is not salvageable;

❖ The actual reason for the breakup;

❖ What other men are part of your children's lives (for example, is their father in the picture?);

❖ Whether the kids are pretty resilient or super-sensitive.

Bear in mind that the kids are likely to feel echoes of your divorce in this situation. Once again, a male adult they had some degree of attachment to has vanished from their lives. Of course, they weren't likely as attached to him as they were to their dad (unless they were extremely young at the time of your divorce). But coming in the wake of your divorce, this situation is likely to impact them harder than a similar loss would under other circumstances.

Make sure they understand that, whatever the reason for the break-up, it wasn't because of them. And if for any reason the kids *were* part of the cause of the breakup? Don't tell them. Plead a need for privacy, or give them other reasons that leave them out of it. They don't need the burden of that responsibility. You could simply tell them, "We want someone who's right for all of us, and he was not that someone."

Assuming the reason had nothing to do with the kids, though, you still don't need to tell them unless the reason is benign and non-personal (maybe he's had a job transfer and must move away). You are entitled to your privacy and can say so if they ask for an explanation.

And as for how to handle their reactions to the breakup, respect their grief or upset, and recognize, too, that in all probability their reactions are in part aftershocks from the divorce. Be sure that whatever other adult males are important in their lives — your brother, father, cousin, youth group leader — are extra-involved with the kids right now, and be sure their presence is felt more strongly for a while.

Although it's rare, it can happen that the man will remain involved in the kids' lives even after you and he break up. Assuming it's not an attempt on his part to try to remain in your life, and assuming the break-up didn't occur because you learned something terrible about him, is there any reason not to let the kids continue spending time with him on occasion? Let us tell you a nice story.

The daughter of a friend of ours attended preschool, quite some time ago, with a boy — let's call him Kevin — whose mom had a relationship that ultimately didn't work out. Young Kevin had become quite attached to Steve, his mom's friend. Kevin's father was out of the picture and, for whatever reasons, didn't visit the boy. When Steve and Kevin's mom broke up, they worked out an arrangement for regular visiting days, just as if Steve were a divorced parent. And Steve kept the schedule religiously, to Kevin's great enjoyment and betterment and the mom's complete satisfaction.

Will it work in every case? Of course not. Will it work for you? Only you (and your ex-beau) can determine this. But it's a thought. And it's fun to tell a happy-ending story once in a while!

What About His Kids?

Some of the prospective men in your life will have had experience parenting kids of their own. What if your kids actually like your new beau, but they don't like his kids? Even if those kids don't live with him, but rather with his ex-wife, they're still going to be visiting often enough. Indeed, if you and your gentleman friend get married, they're going to be your kids' new stepsiblings.

Are there ways to bring these kids together so they can get along, and help allow your romance to blossom?

Again, the answer rests in part with the reasons for their dis-affection. Are your kids simply jealous of your guy's kids? Are they resentful at having to share attention? Is it a case not so much of actively disliking the kids, but of merely having nothing in common with them? (If your daughter is fourteen years old and his daughter a "baby" of nine, or your son is a jock and his son a computer nerd with whom he has nothing in common, they simply might not relate.) Or is there something legitimately dislikable about one or more of his kids? Is one of them bullying, mean, snobbish, catty, rude, crude (even by kids' standards), or otherwise seriously unlikable (such as being a liar, a thief, a serious troublemaker)?

If there is something seriously amiss with one of his kids, is this situation a deal-breaker, or is this problem one that can be overcome? (For example, if the child who's a problem is in therapy, his or her behavior might change with time. You might decide that it would be wise to postpone marrying, but that it's not necessary to break off the relationship totally.)

While you can't let your kids' preferences or whims dictate your romantic alliances, a legitimate objection to the man or his kids is not a mere whim. Your task — and it's not an easy one — is to determine how valid their objections are and act accordingly. Will you proceed with the romance anyhow, proceed cautiously but postpone blending your families for now, or break it off entirely?

If there is something about the man or his kids that's truly tough to take, and you go ahead and marry him anyhow, you will *not* live "happily ever after." No matter how much you love him, if your kids and his are constantly at each other's throat, there will be no peace or happiness in the family. Or if he and your kids constantly clash, you will find yourself in the middle, torn in your allegiances internally and being pulled in two different directions externally. This is not a recipe for a happy outcome.

Maura met Roy and was quickly drawn to him. They dated for about a month before she introduced him to her kids. By this time, she already knew that he was someone special, someone she hoped would remain in her life. She wanted to see how he got along with her sons, Joel and Ryan.

To Maura's delight, Joel and Ryan liked Roy from the first. And Roy seemed to genuinely like the kids too. While continuing to date Roy one-on-one, Maura increasingly also made dates with Roy that included the kids. The four of them went to the movies, the video arcade, and the softball practice field in the local park. They stayed home as a foursome and watched rented movies. And when the circus came to town, they all attended it together.

Roy's kids and their mother lived out of town, though Roy was expecting the kids for a visit soon and also told Maura that his ex was considering a move that would have her living nearby. She wanted Roy more involved in their sons' lives. The older boy, Sean, Roy admitted, was a little tough for his mom to handle alone.

That might have been a red flag for Maura, but she ignored it.

When the boys came for their visit, Maura could see why Roy's ex would have problems with Sean. He was mean, bullying, and cruel. He hurt Roy's dog, and he was none too nice to Maura's sons, especially Ryan, the younger boy, who was less able to defend himself.

Still, Maura made the best of the situation, trying to be warm and caring to both boys and to quell her sons' complaints about Sean. She urged them both to be nice to Sean as well as to his brother. "He won't be here for long," she told them, trying to put a happy face on the situation.

Sean and his brother went home at the end of the week, and a month later, Roy proposed to Maura. She accepted with delight. They set a date for six months later. When three of those six months had elapsed, Roy's ex announced that she was moving back to the area so that the boys could be near their father and Roy could be more actively involved with his sons.

Maura's sons met the news with dismay, but Maura herself put on a bright, determined attitude and exhorted the boys to help her welcome Roy's sons. "Once they have their dad around, he'll see to it that they behave," she stated.

She was being an optimist. No one could make Sean behave. A truly disturbed kid, he stole money from his dad. Then one weekend, when Roy and his sons had been spending a great deal of time at Maura's house, Joel announced that he was missing money from his room.

Despite all the warning signals, Maura went ahead with the wedding. Once they were married, Roy's kids' weekend visits were now at Maura's house. Things went from bad to worse. Sean bullied both Ryan and Joel, totally disrespecting both their property and their rights, and was impossible for Roy to handle. It hardly mattered that his brother was a sweet, giving and caring child. Sean was a serious problem.

Soon Ryan was resentful of Roy for bringing Sean into the household, while Joel turned sullen toward Maura, blaming her for the situation. The family situation deteriorated. Nobody seemed to get along with anyone. Roy put Sean into therapy, but the results of therapy are hardly instant for a child with the deeply ingrained problems Sean had. Meanwhile Maura's family was being torn apart — not only her relationship with her two boys, but with Roy as well.

Eventually Maura divorced Roy, but by then, substantial damage had been done to her relationship with her boys.

What should Maura have done? To begin with, she should *not* have ignored the danger signals that were clearly there before the marriage. And she should not have gone ahead with the wedding as planned. That's not to say she necessarily should have broken it off with Roy when Sean demonstrated what a problem he was, or when he first moved back to town. But she should have at least postponed the marriage. She could have set limits from the outset that might have minimized the damage Sean could cause (such as requiring that Roy supervise him closely when he was at Maura's house or with her kids).

She could have continued to date Roy if she wished but held off marrying him until she saw a significant change in Sean's behavior. Had she done so, she might have salvaged the relationship with Roy as well as avoided the damage she did to her relationship with her own boys. Or, if she decided Sean's behavior was simply intolerable and not likely to get better soon, she could have regretfully broken it off with Roy. But by plowing ahead with the wedding plans and putting a foolish "happy face" on things, she set up a situation in which failure was virtually inevitable. It was a lose/lose situation — nobody came out ahead.

Who Wins This Game?

When divorced parents are dating, the game is fraught with hazards. Kids have their own needs, and a new partner for Mom may or may not be one of them. Bringing a new man into the family's life is a complex and delicate process, with many angles to be considered. It's tough enough to find someone attractive and available to you; then you have to be sure he fits through the very small opening your kids offer.

The key elements in this process are sensitivity to your kids' needs and awareness throughout the process that their needs will become more important with time.

It's hard not to fall in love with someone just because you think your kids may not get along with him. Few of us have that kind of control over our emotions! Yet, it's vital that you keep it in mind.

As you read over this chapter and the previous one again, we invite you to make note of how you might use this information to create a checklist in your mind against which to evaluate prospective male partners. Meanwhile, however, go out with some interesting men. Enjoy dating, and even allow yourself a few "transitional" relationships. If your children see you happy and enthusiastic, it may be harder for them to say, "He's not the right one, Mom."

And who knows, he may be.

AfterWords — Chapter Fourteen

Key Points in the Chapter

- When you decide to begin dating again, don't be surprised if your children oppose the idea.

- Remember, most kids want Mom and Dad to get back together.

- Don't bring every date home to meet the kids. Wait until the relationship appears promising.

- Acknowledge, accept, and tolerate your kids' negative reactions to your dates — then be firm with them and do what feels right to you.

- If it turns out the kids love him and you don't, it's okay to allow them ongoing contact with him.

- Do your kids and his kids get along? That's an important factor in the long-term success of your relationship. Don't overlook it.

Activity of the Week

- If you're ready to start dating, or if you're already involved, plan a discussion with your kids (those who are old enough) about what you like in a man and what they like. Don't lead them to believe they have a "veto" in your romantic relationships, but give them a chance to give you their ideas. You may be surprised at their insights!

Suggested Readings and Resources

Berry, D.B. (1998). *The Divorce Recovery Sourcebook*. Los Angeles: Lowell House.

Browne, J. (1997). *Dating for Dummies*. New York: For Dummies/ Wiley.

Ellis, A. and Crawford, T. (2000). *Making Intimate Connections: Seven Guidelines for Great Relationships and Better Communication*. Atascadero, CA: Impact Publishers.

Fisher, B. and Hart, N. (2000). *Loving Choices: An Experience in Growing Relationships*. Atascadero, CA: Impact Publishers.

15

• • • • • • • • • •

To Marry Again . . . or Not?

A T A WEDDING CYNTHIA ATTENDED a few years ago, when the bride prepared to throw the bouquet, all the single women fled the immediate area. *Nobody* wanted to catch it. The clear implication was that not one of them wanted to get married!

In the "old days," women from their late teens on dated men almost entirely in order to find a husband. Any man who didn't propose after a "reasonable" length of time was considered either "hopeless" or worse, and any woman "stuck" in such a relationship was "wasting her time."

We hardly have to tell you that times have changed, and certainly in this regard. Not every relationship is presumed to be a prelude to marriage just because it survives a reasonable length of time, and not every woman is "marriage-minded." Some women never marry, by choice, and others, having been married once, say, "Been there, done that," and happily go on dating one or more men with no thoughts of marrying either that man or anyone else. Others find living together without benefit of a license from the state to be a comfortable lifestyle.

Yet there are certainly still plenty of women who do want to marry — or remarry — and whose goal is that trip down the aisle to the altar.

"I'll Never Get Married Again!"

Of course, there are plenty of women who have no intention of marrying again but then meet "Mr. Right" and change their minds about their futures.

Though Holly's divorce itself was not a particularly unpleasant one, the marriage it terminated had been a bitter disappointment to her. Cody's flaws as a husband were many, and Holly was left feeling that she had the worst of both worlds: She wasn't enjoying all the good things she'd expected in a marriage, such as emotional support, intellectual stimulation, companionship, reliable and safe sexual satisfaction, and a partner who brought in a steady income (as she did). Holly initiated many conversations with Cody about what she felt was lacking in the marriage, but these always turned into confrontations, bitter arguing, and no changes. Counseling failed to resolve the problems either, and finally Holly filed for divorce.

The marriage had lasted seven years. By mutual consent the couple was childless, and they lived in a rental apartment, so Cody didn't contest the few things Holly asked for in the settlement. Thus, the actual divorce process was relatively painless. But Holly was left with a bad taste for marriage after the "fiasco" (to use her word) that her marriage had turned out to be. She resolved to stay single thereafter.

At first she didn't date at all, preferring the company of her friends (including some platonic male friends). Eventually she met Raymond, who was pleasant and easy to be with, and was no more marriage-minded than was Holly. They began dating casually, seeing each other on weekends, and enjoying each other's company.

The relationship endured on that same casual level for nearly a year. Raymond then met someone he was seriously taken with. He took Holly out for one last dinner, and told her frankly about his new romance. He explained that he wanted to be straight with both Holly and the new woman in his life, and had concluded that he needed to break up with Holly and focus entirely on his new love. If Holly ever needed his help or friendship, he said, he'd be there for her.

Holly was appreciative of the way Raymond handled the situation. Though disappointed, she wasn't really emotionally invested in the relationship, so she felt no serious pangs at his announcement. They reminisced about some of the funnier things that had happened to them during the time they'd been dating. When Holly kissed Raymond good-night for the last time, she wished him luck and love and meant every word she said.

But, having become accustomed to having a man to spend weekends with, Holly found herself missing Raymond's companionship. She still was convinced she'd never marry again, but she found herself wishing there were a man — a *casual* relationship, but a relationship all the same — in her life. Quite a contrast to her feelings in the wake of her marriage, when she hadn't even cared if she dated or not.

One evening her friend Bette called: "I met a guy at work this afternoon I think you'd really like. I told him I had a friend — you — and he gave me his number. If you're interested, his name is Ted." Holly took the number.

Holly and Ted didn't feel any sparks when they met for drinks, but Ted said that *he* had a friend he thought would be perfect for Holly. Ted was a nice enough guy, and Holly was in an adventurous mood, so she agreed and gave Ted her phone number to give to his friend, Clay.

Clay turned out to be clever, witty, caring, dynamic, a research scientist who was enamored of his work and made it sound fascinating. Holly found herself attentive and interested, though she'd usually found science boring in the past. She was quite taken with Clay and was glad when he asked if he could see her again.

Soon they were going out several times a week and, after a few months of dating, the relationship became quite intense. They began seeing each other virtually every night and spending many nights together — de facto living together, though they maintained separate residences. "Isn't this silly?" Clay pointed out. "We ought to make it official and save on the mortgage payments... though that's hardly my main reason. I know how I feel about you."

"You mean live together?" Holly asked.

"Well...that would be okay, I guess, but what I really meant was marriage. I love you, Holly. I have no interest in anyone else, and I'd like to spend the rest of my life with you. I kinda hoped you felt the same way...."

Holly was dumbstruck. Finally she said, "Why don't we try living together first?"

"In case you haven't noticed, we already are," Clay said drily.

One of the things that Holly found attractive in Clay to begin with was her ability to talk to him about serious matters and his ability to listen — *really* listen — and to give thoughtful advice. So finally she opened up to him about her feelings about marriage: How it had been a disaster the first time around, how she had no great desire to repeat that mistake, how she saw no real reason to get married again, particularly in light of the fact that she had no desire to have kids.

Clay listened carefully, then told her he certainly didn't want her to do anything that would make her uncomfortable. "But am I the same person your ex was?" he asked.

Holly yelped, "Of course not!"

"Then why do you think marriage with me would be the same as marriage with him?"

They continued to discuss the subject, for the most part calmly. Clay was analytical, as usual, and Holly followed his reasoning. "But why is marriage necessary?" she asked at one point. "Why not just combine our households and live together officially instead of as-good-as, like we are now?"

"We could," Clay agreed. "But why *not* get married? Do you think you're going to want to back out of our relationship in a year? If you do, we shouldn't even combine households."

"No. I love you," Holly said. "I don't want to leave you. Or lose you."

"Then why not go the whole nine yards with the minister and the rings and the whole ceremony? Don't answer that! Just think about it." And he changed the subject. They didn't discuss it further that evening.

But Holly gave it lots of thought. *Why not?* she thought. Clay was nothing like her ex. Marriage to Clay would be nothing like her former marriage. Sure, it wasn't important to her to get married again, but, since she loved Clay, and since he was a totally different kind of man from her ex, was there any reason she shouldn't get married again?

In the end, she decided that "cold feet" was the only reason...and not a good one.

They got married and, at last report, were still very happy together.

There are plenty of women who are reluctant to try marriage a second time when the first time didn't work. Some, like Holly, change their minds when they meet the right man. Some eventually move into committed, live-together relationships, minus the rings. And some remain perpetually single, by choice or by chance — or both.

Why Do Divorcées Remarry?

Of those divorced women who want to marry again, some have better reasons than others. Do any of these apply to you?

❖ *You've found a man you really love, and you want to formalize your commitment.*

(This is one of the most traditional and rational reasons for marrying.)

❖ *You really love each other and want to live together, and for moral or religious reasons, or because you have kids, you're not comfortable living together unmarried.*

(This is a very solid reason.)

❖ *You've found someone you love, and you don't want to let him get away.*

(This is a marriage born of insecurity rather than true commitment.)

❖ *You're a traditionalist and feel women should be married.*

(Social tradition alone is not a strong basis for marriage, but this is a semi-OK reason to remarry, provided you don't marry the wrong person just to avoid remaining single.)

❖ *You want to have children, and you want them to be born to married parents.*

(This is a reasonable position, if, once again, you don't marry the wrong person solely to have children.)

❖ *You have children from your last marriage and want a man in their lives whom they can look up to, emulate (if they're boys), and love and rely on.*

(This is a good reason to want to remarry, but be careful to choose a man who will be both a good stepdad to your kids and a good husband to you as well.)

❖ *You have children from your last marriage and want help in raising them.*

(This is not a sound basis for marriage. If this is your only reason for marrying, it puts you in a position of weakness. If it's one of a number of reasons, it's an OK stance to take.)

❖ *You want the greater financial ease that an additional income will give you.*

(Greater financial ease may be one of the benefits of marriage, but it should not be your primary objective in marrying. Financial conditions can change, and jobs can be lost. He has to bring more into your life than money if you want a good marriage.)

❖ *You don't want to go through life always concerned about who you can invite to go with you to parties and other events where most people will be in couples.*

(Not a good basis for marriage. You would be better off to find a male friend who can be your "steady partner" for such events.)

❖ *You don't want to look like a loser who can't get a man.*

(Worrying what other people will think is never a good reason... for anything.)

❖ *You hope that having a husband will help fend off the advances of your ex, or other wolves.*

(It may or may not achieve that, but it's a poor reason to get married.)

❖ *You want reliable companionship.*

(Provided it's part of a package deal that heavily features love, this is a reasonable position.)

❖ You want a steady partner for sex.

(Same comment as above.)

❖ *You want the full benefits of marriage for you and your partner. Hospitals and government agencies consult only a legal spouse on vital decisions.*

(One good reason for marrying, rather than just living with, someone you already love.)

❖ *Your parents (or other relatives) are hounding you to remarry.*

(You can't — and shouldn't — live your life to please your parents.)

❖ *You want a man to complete you.*

(You need to learn to complete yourself. Ultimately, you have only yourself to rely on.)

❖ *You want to live "happily ever after."*

(Fairy tale romances exist only in fairy tales. Women who expect Cinderella marriages are setting themselves up for disappointment. The best of marriages still have bumps in the road.)

The point of all this is to examine your motives for wanting to get married, whether you're contemplating marrying a particular man you've been seeing, or whether you're on the hunt for a suitable man to marry.

For Your Own Reasons

If, on the other hand, you're sure you *don't* want to get married again, you probably aren't ready for marriage and shouldn't let anyone else push you into it. You may simply not have healed enough yet. You may be ready and willing six months from now, or perhaps not for three years. Jumping right into a new marriage shortly after the dissolution of your previous marriage is a bad idea in any case.

How long should you wait? While there's no one set time, professional opinion suggests at least a year, maybe two. More important than the calendar is whether you've done the work of divorce recovery described in chapter 2. Get your own life together before you marry again. Climb that "mountain" Bruce Fisher talked about. Base your new marriage on the solid foundation of your own emotional strength. Don't marry out of neediness.

Some other factors to consider:

❖ Your personality

❖ How bad your marriage was

❖ How long your marriage lasted

❖ How nasty the divorce was.

The woman who leaves an unsatisfactory — but not horrible — marriage with a minimum of rancor, or the woman who ends a marriage after just six months or three years because she realizes the marriage was a mistake, is going to recover a lot faster — perhaps in a year. If, however, she was devastated by the termination of her marriage, or if she was married for thirty years, or if her marriage was a horror story that has left her embittered and/or suspicious, she'll take longer to put her life back together — maybe three years (or more?).

Whatever your own situation, doing your emotional recovery work before you take that trip down the aisle again will make a huge difference in your success the second time around.

On the Rebound — Do Transitional Romances Work Out?

Does that mean that a divorced woman can't fall in love a short time after the dissolution of her marriage? No, it doesn't mean that, but be advised: most often, these "rebound relationships" don't last. And why should they? Isn't the point here to allow new men into your life to help you move on to a future good life? While you're in transition between your lost love and a new permanent partnership, you'll want to take advantage of opportunities to learn all you can about what you really want from a new relationship.

Are *all* rebound relationships doomed to failure? Of course not...but most are. Too often the love — or what feels like love — is ill-founded. Two of the most common explanations are:

❖ The woman is used to being half a couple and falls for the first man she meets with whom she thinks she might be happy.

❖ The woman who was miserable in her marriage meets a man who treats her well and helps her feel good about herself — and him. She is grateful, and she mistakes that feeling for love.

It's not unusual to find, when you've barely gotten out of one relationship, that you feel like you're "in love" again. And you may be, temporarily. After all, it's been a while since you've allowed someone other than your ex to make you the center of his attention and affection. It's flattering, and feels really good. But, as you know by now, there's a lot more to it than that!

We've mentioned before that Bruce Fisher liked to say that "relationships are our teachers." His counsel: develop "growing relationships" and take time to learn all you can about yourself as a romantic partner before you get serious about a new love. Transitional romances are usually temporary; they occasionally grow into lasting partnerships, but don't count on it!

The best advice we can give you is, if you're out of your former marriage less than a year and meet someone you think you want to marry, postpone setting a wedding date till at least a year has elapsed. If it's true love and solidly grounded, it won't change or go away while you wait. And if you *have* rushed into something on less than solid ground, it's easier to extricate yourself before you've tied the marriage knot than after. You know that from experience!

Why not set a date but make it for some time after a year? Is that your question? Because once you've set a date, you're under a great deal of pressure to carry through with the plans. Yes, you can still cancel the wedding. But, whether it was to be a quiet ceremony with four friends in front of a court clerk, or a huge, lavish wedding with three hundred guests, caterers, a live band, and a hired hall, it's still more difficult to tell your friends, your family, and — above all — your fiancé that you've changed your mind once the date has been set. So consider a long engagement, if you're sure you want to get engaged, but don't set a date.

And, meanwhile, keep climbing!

Shall We Move in Together and See How It Goes?

What about living together? Is that a feasible interim step?

If you're too recently out of a marriage to jump into another one, or too unsure or hesitant to recommit, moving in together is certainly a less binding step than marriage. But it's a lot like marriage, and it's still a huge risk. If, two or five or eight months down the line, you decide that this isn't working out, you don't really love him, he's got the same faults as your ex, he has a totally different slate of faults but they're equally intolerable, or you realize you're simply not ready, you're going to have to divide up your assets and start over. Even if you've kept separate bank accounts, who gets the bed, the toaster oven, the TV, the dishes, and — most of all — who gets to stay put and who has to look for a new home?

On the other hand, living together could easily be a prelude to marriage, if all of the following conditions apply to you:

... the issue isn't that it's a rebound relationship but merely that you have cold feet, *and*

... you'd like to ease back into the water instead of plunging, *and*

... merging households without making it legal makes you feel more comfortable, *and*

... you're sure you really love him, *and*

... he loves you, *and*

... you truly believe you could live happily together.

You can always plan a marriage later on... or you may find that simply living together suits you both just fine.

Should You Ever Remarry Your Ex?

Hardly ever.

But then again, "ever" is an awfully heavy word. There are exceptions to most rules, and certainly there are exceptional cases in which two divorced former spouses reunite and make it work the second time. But they're going to have to have done some serious growing and changing between Marriage Number One and Marriage Number Two. Otherwise nothing is different — promises and entreaties notwithstanding. And if nothing is different within the emotional makeup of the two people, nothing is going to be different in the marriage. It's on a path to self-destruct again.

However, it's not hopeless. *If...*

... there have been some real personality changes (through therapy or a divorce recovery process, or serious personal growth on their own), *and*

... the partners have differing expectations of what the marriage will bring this time, *and*

... they have truly changed within,

then yes, there is some hope it will work a second time. But most re-marriages between ex-spouses fail the second time for the same reasons they failed the first time.

Familiarity can be appealing, and you don't have to go through the process of meeting and vetting new candidates for your affection. But, unless there are serious changes in both of you, we can't offer an optimistic prognosis.

Should You Consider Remarrying
If You've Been Divorced Twice Already?

Consider it? You might. Should you think very hard about it before taking that big step? You'd better!

There are few failed marriages in which the blame lies squarely on just one half of the couple. (Certainly cases in which the husband is abusive or is a cheater would be among the exceptions.) But even when the fault *was* primarily or totally the husband's, if the wife marries someone abusive or someone with a "zipper problem" *twice*, she's exhibiting either poor judgment or a tendency to be drawn to that type of person, or both — which doesn't bode well for a third try.

Again, if she's been through therapy or has otherwise done some serious growing and changing, the woman might select a more suitable partner next time. (There's another vote for learning about yourself through transitional relationships!) Otherwise, she'll likely be drawn to a similar personality and find herself in a marriage with a man no less flawed than her first two husbands were.

And if it's not so cut-and-dried as a case of the husband being an abuser or an alcoholic or a cheater? Then likely there was fault on both sides, and the wife deserves to bear some weight for the failed marriage. If that's the case, the second failed marriage raises the question: *Is she repeating her mistakes?*

Even if the husband's flaws in the second marriage were different from those of the first husband, they might be reactions to the same behavior in her. Example: The wife is shrill and argumentative. Husband Number One reacted by arguing back, and ultimately they divorced because of constant verbal fights. Husband Number Two reacted to her behavior differently: by withdrawing more and more, and ultimately failing to communicate. She finally divorced him because he had retreated from the marriage. It *appears* that she had a different problem with the second husband than with the first. But in actuality, the two disparate problems were the two husbands' differing ways of reacting to the same behavior in her.

The Bottom Line

So, should you remarry? If you want to, and for the right reasons, and if you're not freshly out of your last marriage, and if you don't have a suspect track record. If you're too recently out of your last marriage, get engaged if you must, but postpone the nuptials or even setting a date. And if you have a past history of plural divorces, you'd better do some serious soul-searching before deciding to take the aisle-walk again.

For that matter, even if you've been divorced only once, some soul-searching is important. *Why* did your last marriage fail? If you feel it was his fault, can you point to any behavior on your part that might have led him to behave as he did?

If he was a cheater, is it really that he has a zipper problem, or did you do anything — or fail to do something — that led him to another woman's bed? It's not just a wife being cold in bed that can lead a man to stray. People who seek sex outside of marriage are often really looking for something else: affection, conversation, companionship, validation.

If he was a substance abuser, did that behavior come with the package, or did it begin during your marriage? "She drove him to drink" is an old saw, but it has some truth to it. We know that cuts both ways, of course.

If he was the one to end the marriage, what reason(s) did he give? It's true that sometimes people just grow apart and, once the kids are gone, find there's nothing really holding them together anymore, but if that's the case, the marriage that should have been worked on long before this.

We're not trying to discourage you from remarrying. Far from it! We just want to make sure that, if you do remarry, you build your next marriage on a solid foundation, marry the right man for the right reasons, and don't give *him* any reason to want to leave *you*.

Will It Ever Be Perfect?

And if you do marry again? Can you expect sunshine and roses to follow you for the rest of your lives? Of course not!

Women with Cinderella expectations are often dismayed the first time they have a dispute or misunderstanding with their husbands. But couples disagree. And one argument does not spell divorce, or mean "he doesn't love me anymore." If you are happy and satisfied within the marriage most of the time, and he respects you and treats you well, you're ahead of the game.

But even before you get to the first argument, you're going to have a period of adjustment. (This is less true if you lived together for a while before you married.) If you wake up chipper and chirpy, while he needs an hour and two full pots of coffee to get going, he may well resent your bright-eyed cheeriness, or you may find his slow starts tough to deal with. Are you someone who gets easily bugged by a person who leaves the toothpaste cap off — and he does just that?

We know a couple with a "sleep disorder." She often wakes in the middle of the night and, unable to get back to sleep, tries to read herself to sleep. He soon wakes up, finds the light disturbing, is unable to get back to sleep, and gets terribly annoyed at what he perceives as her inherent thoughtlessness. (Sometimes the "fix" is easy and obvious. In this case, a tiny clip-on light would allow her to read without bothering him.)

And of course, if either of you has children still at home, there will be even more adjustments needed as the kids get used to their new stepparent and any new stepsiblings. But that's a topic for not just another chapter but a whole other book. (Check the Resources list at the end of this chapter.)

There are plenty of second marriages that work. The two applicable questions are:

❖ Have you examined *honestly and fairly* the causes of your first marriage's failure? Do you see whatever part you played in the failure, whether these were acts of commission (things you did that you shouldn't have), acts of omission (things you should have done but didn't), or errors in judgment (being attracted to the wrong type of man, or thinking, "I know he's wrong for me, but I love him," or "I know there are things about him that seriously bug me, but I'll change him after we're married")?

❖ Have you *grown and changed* since your first marriage, so that you won't repeat your mistakes, flaws, or other damaging behaviors or expectations that might have contributed to the downfall of your first marriage?

If you can honestly answer "Yes" to both these questions, you have an awfully good shot at making a much better go of your next marriage than your last one.

Do you *want* to get married? Only you can answer that. *Should* you get married? Only if you really want to and you're sure you're ready. Will it work out this time? Well, if...

... you've paid attention to this chapter, *and*

... you're marrying for good reasons, *and*

... you've let enough time elapse since your divorce that you're not moving precipitously, *and*

... you're not entering this relationship with raw emotional wounds, *and*

... you've identified your part in the previous marriage's failure, *and*

... you've completed the steps of your own divorce recovery process,

you have a really good chance.

We wish you luck... and love.

AfterWords — Chapter Fifteen

Key Points in the Chapter

- Second marriages have a much better chance of working out if the partners have worked through the full divorce recovery process (such as the steps outlined in chapter two).

- If you want to marry again, it's important to wait a year or two after your divorce. You need time to do the recovery work, and to become an independent person, before you enlist for a new tour.

- There are many good reasons — and some not very good ones — for wanting to marry again. Be sure yours are your own, and that they are the good ones!

- Transitional relationships can be great opportunities to learn about yourself and your expectations for future long-term commitments. Rarely however, do they work out for the long term.

- Living together can tell you a lot about each other, but marriages that follow living together are no more successful — statistically — than others.

- If you remarry your ex, don't expect things to change much.

- Build your new marriage on a solid foundation of your growth toward independence, avoiding mistakes of the past, honesty, and equality.

Activity of the Week

- If you're considering remarriage, take out that journal and write yourself a letter — better yet, an essay — discussing the mistakes you made in your previous love relationship. Describe what attracted you to him, what you learned about him — and about yourself — while you were married, what led to the divorce, what patterns of behavior you found unacceptable in him, and — most important — how you've changed so you won't go down the same road again.

Suggested Readings and Resources

Carlson, J. and Dinkmeyer, D. (2002). *Time for a Better Marriage.* Atascadero, CA: Impact Publishers.

Ellis, A. and Crawford, T. (2000). *Making Intimate Connections: Seven Guidelines for Great Relationships and Better Communication.* Atascadero, CA: Impact Publishers.

Fisher, B. and Alberti, R.E. (2000). *Rebuilding: When Your Relationship Ends* (third edition). Atascadero, CA: Impact Publishers.

Fisher, B. and Hart, N. (2000). *Loving Choices: An Experience in Growing Relationships.* Atascadero, CA: Impact Publishers.

Afterword

WHERE DOES THIS READING FIND YOU in your post-marriage life?

Contemplating a divorce?

Filing the dreaded paperwork?

Waiting for the attorneys to thrash out who-gets-what?

Recently divorced and wondering how you're going to cope?

Struggling with this new stage of your life and all its problems and new situations?

Thinking about dating again and wondering if there are any good men out there?

Dating again and wondering about how to separate the wheat from the chaff?

Contemplating remarriage and wondering if this time around you'll have better success?

Wherever you are in the continuum that began with the end of your marriage, you're in the midst of a new time in your life. One that's full of unique problems and obstacles....

But you're also at the beginning of something. You're at the beginning of the next phase of your life and your renewed chance for some real happiness.

You may find that happiness lies in living alone (or alone with your kids) and enjoying your independence. Lots of divorced women discover that there is life without marriage. You may find that happiness will ultimately result from a love relationship — marital or otherwise — with someone far better suited to you than was your ex-husband. You may enjoy independence for a while and then connect with that wonderful someone.

Along the way, you have a chance to reap some great fringe benefits. In the course of finding new interests, new friends, and a new life, you may choose to return to school to get that college degree you gave up on years ago. You may seek out a new and much more rewarding career, or start your own successful business. You may make some wonderful new friends. You may become intrigued by some great new hobbies, volunteer activities, or other pursuits.

You're going to experience some major personal growth as you meet the challenges of divorce. You're going to find yourself growing as you honestly examine your role in the ending of your marriage, and as you work to correct the flaws or foibles on your part that may have contributed to the divorce. You're going to grow as you work your way through the process of divorce recovery and rebuilding your life. And you're going to grow as you discover you can manage life on your own.

Does it sound as if we're saying, "Every cloud has a silver lining"? Or perhaps, "Everything turns out for the best"? Well, we're not going to go that far. Certainly not *every* cloud, and not *everything*. But there are reasons those hackneyed expressions have endured for decades. Life can change, and we fallible, vulnerable humans can bring about change in our lives. You can literally create the good life for yourself. And you can do it on your own.

We hope this book has helped — and will continue to help — as you make your way. Put it where you can easily find it again when you want to reread it. Perhaps when you need a little emotional support, or when you're looking for answers to specific situations we may have discussed. Maybe when you find yourself in the next phase of the post-divorce process and want a quick reminder of the problems and pitfalls to expect. Or maybe just as an occasional "refresher course."

We wish you a path that's not too rocky. We wish you strength in meeting your challenges successfully. And above all, we wish you happiness and fulfillment in your new good life.

After Your Divorce

APPENDICES

APPENDIX I

· · · · · · · · · · · · · · ·

Safer Sex

E ven though "safer sex" and the need to adhere to it may be awkward or uncomfortable to discuss, it is extremely important to have this conversation with potential sexual partners. You need to make it clear that you will not do anything risky. Risky behaviors include such activities as engaging in sex without the protection of a condom. One alternative to condom usage is restricting your activities to alternative, non-entry sex, such as mutual masturbation or what you may have called, in your younger days, "the dry grind." And you need to try to evaluate how much of a risk your potential partner poses, since condoms, while they provide the most protection possible, are not one-hundred percent foolproof. Of course, your new lover or would-be lover is not likely to tell you that he falls into a higher-risk category (such as bisexual, intravenous drug user, or promiscuous bed-hopper), but if you listen to his conversations and "read between the lines," you may be able to make some determination as to whether you seem to hear any danger signals. Please remember, too, that cleanliness is *not an indicator* that a person is free of HIV/AIDS (or any other STD). While good hygiene is certainly desirable in a sexual partner, it is in no way a protection against HIV/AIDS or other STDs.

Take control of your life in the area of sexuality, and make careful choices that reflect the respect you have for yourself, your health, and your life. Never was the old adage "Better to be safe than sorry" more appropriate.

Impact Publishers, which publishes a number of books on relationships and divorce (including this book and others in the Rebuilding Books series), has prepared the following statement regarding sensible safer sex. We encourage you to read it and to consider carefully how it may apply in your life.

Impact Publishers Statement on Safer Sex

Impact Publishers, Inc. recognizes safe and healthy approaches to sexual expression as one of the principal health and social issues of our time. We offer the following statement for your serious consideration:

❖ Sexual expression is a basic, normal, positive, intensely personal and highly satisfying human activity. Although sexual practices are often publicly regulated by social mores, religious values, and law, individuals and couples decide privately how they will live their sex lives.

❖ In addition to important choices about personal moral values, responsible sexual practice requires good information, including knowledge of the fundamentals of human sexuality, responsible family planning, contraceptive choices, and protection against sexually transmitted diseases.

❖ Sexually transmitted diseases, such as Acquired Immune Deficiency Syndrome (AIDS), Chlamydia, various forms of Herpes, Hepatitis B, and the several other Sexually Transmitted Diseases, are serious and widespread public health problems, both in the United States and throughout the populated world.

❖ "Safer sex" — minimizing the risks of sexually transmitted diseases — includes at minimum the following:
  – an absolutely certain, long-term, exclusively monogamous relationship between two partners who have tested negative for HIV infection, or ALL of the following:
  – regular periodic physical examinations;
  – conscientious, unfailing use of condoms (preferably with spermicides) during intercourse;
  – awareness and avoidance of common risk factors in STDs (e.g., sex with members of high-risk populations including but not limited to intravenous drug users,);
  – honest and open discussion of sexual habits and preferences with potential partners;
  – infrequent changing of partners.

❖ Each individual — married or single — has the right to freedom of choice in sexual expression, so long as the practice involves consenting adults and consciously avoids physical or psychological harm to any person.

❖ No one is obligated to have a sexual relationship with another person — including a marriage partner — unless he or she wishes to do so.

❖ The following AIDS facts are adapted from the brochure, *Understanding AIDS: A Message from the Surgeon General* [a U.S. government publication]:

- *Who you are has nothing to do with whether you are in danger of being infected with the AIDS virus. What matters is what you do.*

- *There are two main ways you can get AIDS. First, you can become infected by having sex — oral, anal, or vaginal — with someone who is infected with the AIDS virus. Second, you can be infected by sharing drug needles and syringes with an infected person.*

- *Your chances of coming into contact with the virus increase with the number of sex partners you have.*

- *You won't get AIDS through everyday contact...a mosquito bite ...saliva, sweat, tears, urine, or a bowel movement...a kiss ...clothes, a telephone, or from a toilet seat.*

- *A person can be infected with the AIDS virus without showing any symptoms at all.*

- *The AIDS virus may live in the human body for years before actual symptoms appear.*

- *Condoms are the best preventative measure against AIDS besides not having sex and practicing safe behavior.*

- *RISKY BEHAVIOR*

   Sharing drug needles and syringes.

   Anal sex, with or without a condom.

   Vaginal or oral sex with someone who shoots drugs or engages in anal sex.

   Sex with someone you don't know well (a pickup or prostitute) or with someone you know has several sex partners.

   Unprotected sex (without a condom) with an infected person.

- *SAFE BEHAVIOR*

   Not having sex.

   Sex with one mutually faithful, uninfected partner.

   Not shooting drugs.

- *If you know someone well enough to have sex, then you should be able to talk about AIDS. If someone is unwilling to talk, you shouldn't have sex.*

APPENDIX II

. . . .

Would It Help
to See a Therapist?

Issues To Consider

The following are questions to consider in deciding to seek psychotherapy.

❖ Are there life-threatening issues (strong thoughts about suicide, self-harm, or impulses to hurt/abuse others)? If you honestly answer yes, please call a professional today.

❖ Are there major stress-related physical symptoms causing noticeable discomfort? Examples of such symptoms include:

- Sleep disturbances

- Pronounced weight loss or weight gain

- Severe daytime fatigue

- Headaches

- Poor concentration and memory; forgetfulness; an inability to keep focused or pay attention

- Inability to recover normally from physical illnesses (when your physician has determined emotional stress to be a contributing factor)

❖ Are emotional problems seriously interfering with functioning in daily life? For example: missing work or school, inability to care for the needs of your children, unsafe driving due to poor concentration or extreme anxiety.

❖ Are emotional problems leading to significant abuse of alcohol or other substances?

❖ Do you simply not have the social support network to provide help during hard times? A supportive family, close friends, a church or community group — all can contribute to effective healing if they are willing and able to listen; however, such people may not be there for you to turn to.

It is also important to note that friends and family may not be willing to support change and growth. At such times, the other person may genuinely care for or love you, but may also have an investment in maintaining the status quo. Even very positive change and growth are often difficult for others to understand and accept. A therapist may be able to provide support for change when others can't.

❖ Are there emotional issues that are simply too private to discuss with friends or family members?

❖ Are you doing all you can to cope and to heal but simply feel overwhelmed or especially stuck?

Should you at this point be thinking that psychotherapy may be helpful but you're still on the fence, consider the following three issues:

❖ Am I fooling myself by believing "Oh, it's not that big a deal...I can cope with this...I just need to try harder"? Denial is a common human tendency. Many people, if honest with themselves, are suffering tremendously and yet feel compelled to minimize or deny the truth of their own inner feelings. Denial may be a short-term solution (like trying to deny that you have a bad toothache) but won't serve you well for very long. There is a place for honestly confronting yourself to see if you are trying to cover up genuine emotional pain.

❖ Do I value the quality of my life enough to make emotional healing and growth a priority?

❖ Have I exhausted all my other resources — including an effort to try the approaches described in this book — to no avail?

Selecting a Therapist

If you are considering psychotherapy, selecting the right therapist is very important. Here are three main steps to follow in your search:

❖ Speak with your family doctor, clergyperson, friends, or others who may have contact with the professional community, and collect the names of two or three therapists in your area. In most towns, there will be a handful of therapists with established reputations. The therapist you choose should be well recommended — by two or three people you trust — and should have good credentials (graduate degrees, supervised training, licensure, recognition by professional societies).

❖ Once you have satisfied yourself as to the therapist's recommendations and credentials, the second step is to telephone the therapist to talk about your main reason for seeking therapy now. Obviously, it is impossible to fully explain your life circumstances in a minute or two, but the main reason for doing so on the phone is to see how the therapist responds to you. This initial contact with the therapist is important; it may be possible to get some first impressions. Often people feel anxious about making an appointment. Most therapists understand this anxiety and use this first contact to help put you at ease and tell you something about their practice (e.g., how often they meet with a client, their fees, their specialties, their approach). Two of my main goals in talking to potential patients in advance of the first visit is to help them feel more relaxed about this decision to see me and to express my intent to work together with them.

If you feel reluctant to make an appointment, it is fine simply to call a therapist and talk for a few minutes and possibly share your apprehension about coming in. If you still feel hesitant, remember that when you go to see a therapist, in a real sense, you are hiring him or her to assist you in a professional way. If for any reason you are not comfortable with the person, you don't have to go back. You are in control of that decision at all times.

❖ The third step in your selection process is to evaluate the therapist and the therapy process in general after the initial session. After talking to the therapist during the initial session, you will very likely be able to judge for yourself if this therapy seems to be a good approach for you. The therapist should provide considerable information about his/her approach and why it is appropriate to your needs. There should be an open discussion of such issues as fees, "informed consent," and any limits of confidentiality. You'll also be getting a "feel" for the therapist's personal style in relating to you. Important things to look for during the first session are: "Does the therapist seem to understand me?" and "Do I have a sense of hopefulness about her kind of treatment?" No type of treatment can resolve emotional issues immediately; it will take some time and effort on your part. But if your answers to the two questions are "yes," then you have reason to believe that working with this particular therapist may be beneficial.

Types of Mental Health Therapists

❖ *Psychiatrist (M.D.):* Psychiatrists are medical doctors who have received specialized training in the treatment of emotional problems, including both medication and psychological treatments. (It is possible for a physician to practice psychiatry without specialized training; however, very few do so. Again, it is appropriate to ask about *any* professional's background, training and experience in dealing with conditions like yours.) Most psychiatrists treat emotional disorders with medications. Some psychiatrists also provide psychotherapy, behavior therapy, or cognitive therapy. "Board certification" is an advanced designation granted by the profession to those psychiatrists who are especially well qualified.

❖ *Psychologist:* Psychologists hold doctoral degrees in psychology (Ph. D., Psy.D., Ed.D.), have three or four years of postgraduate training in psychological methods, and in most states, are licensed to practice. They also have specialized training in the administration and interpretation of psychological tests. The most advanced designation for a practicing psychologist is that of "Diplomate" of the American Board of Examiners in Professional Psychology.

❖ *Clinical Social Worker:* Clinical social workers generally hold masters degrees (M.S.W.), have considerable supervised experience and are usually licensed by the state (hence the designation, "L.C.S.W." — Licensed Clinical Social Worker). A nationally recognized certification is "A.C.S.W." — for members of the Academy of Clinical Social Workers.

❖ *Marriage Family and Child Counselors/Therapists:* Some states grant licenses to Marriage, Family and Child Counselors (or Marriage, Family and Child Therapists). Such therapists generally have at least a masters degree in counseling (M.A. or M.S.), usually with specialization in treatment of marriage and family problems or problems of children and adolescents. "Clinical Member" or "Supervisor" designations by the American Association for Marital and Family Therapy are further evidence of qualifications of MFCC's.

❖ *Pastoral Counselors:* Some clergy have received training in counseling and may provide supportive therapy to members of their church or to others desiring a therapist who addresses both emotional and spiritual concerns. A few pastoral counselors are also qualified under one of the categories above.

Adapted from *Survivors: Stories and Strategies to Heal the Hurt,* copyright © 2002, by John Preston, Psy.D. Published by Impact Publishers, Inc., Atascadero, California, and used by permission of the publisher. Further reproduction prohibited under U.S. and international copyright law.

INDEX
· · · · · · · ·

More Books With *Impact*

Your Perfect Right: *Assertiveness and Equality in Your Life and Relationships* **(8th Ed.)**
Robert E. Alberti, Ph.D. and Michael L. Emmons, Ph.D.
Softcover: $15.95   Hardcover: $21.95   256 pages
Eighth edition of the assertiveness book most recommended by psychologists — fifth most recommended among all self-help books! Helps readers step-by-step to develop more effective self-expression.

The Assertive Woman (Fourth Edition)
Stanlee Phelps, M.S.W. and Nancy K. Austin, M.B.A.
Softcover: $15.95   256 pages
Over 400,000 copies sold, the original assertiveness book for women. Already one of the most powerful self-help books ever, this fourth edition is completely revised and up-to-date.

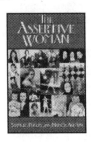

The Stress Owner's Manual: *Meaning, Balance and Health in Your Life* **(2nd Ed.)**
Ed Boenisch, Ph.D. and C. Michele Haney, Ph.D.
Softcover: $15.95   224 pages
New edition of the popular practical guide to stress management with self-assessment charts covering people, money, work, leisure stress areas. Life-changing strategies to enhance relaxation and serenity.

How to Make Yourself Happy and Remarkably Less Disturbable
Albert Ellis, Ph.D.
Softcover: $15.95   224 pages
Dr. Ellis offers simple, straightforward procedures to help you change your disturbing thoughts into healthy ones, make yourself less disturbable in the face of adversity, overcome anxiety, depression, rage, self-hate, or self-pity .